Book Club Groups:

A Multilevel Four-Blocks® Reading Strategy

by
Dorothy P. Hall
and
CeCe Tillman

Carson-Dellosa Publishing Company, Inc.
Greensboro, North Carolina

Credits

Editor
Joey Bland

Layout Design
Jon Nawrocik

Inside Illustrations
Bill Neville

Cover Design
Peggy Jackson

Dedications and Acknowledgements

To Cooper Aidan Hunnicutt, my grandson, a wonderful addition to our family and my life!

Dottie Hall

This book is lovingly dedicated to my family: my mom, Ann, who instilled in me a love of reading; my husband, Billy, who doesn't mind my obsessive habit; and my children, Courtney and Emily. I hope to pass on my love of reading to them.

Many people have shaped my professional life. I would like to take this opportunity to acknowledge just a few of them. Barb Neslin first introduced me to the Four-Blocks® model. Laura Kump and other friends on the Four-Blocks mail ring provided thoughtful support. Pat Cunningham and Dottie Hall welcomed me to the Four-Blocks family. The staff at Davis Elementary gave me the opportunity to practice and refine my skills, which I continue to do with support from Sharon Walpole. The field of education is rich with knowledge and support. My wish is for every educator to be so fortunate.

CeCe Tillman

[Table of Contents]

[Table of Contents]

Book Club Groups: Introduction

" . . . everyone is talking about 'Book Club Groups' . . ."

People have always gotten together and talked about good books. Sometimes, a group of friends read and discuss a favorite book as they pass it from one person to the next. Sometimes, everyone in a group buys the same book, then reads and discusses the book at the same time. Oprah Winfrey made "Book Club Groups" even more popular when she selected a book for all of her viewers to read, then discussed the selection on her television show. Now, it seems that everyone is talking about "Book Club Groups," including schools.

Some schools choose a book for a parent to read with a group of students, then the parent leads a discussion of the book with the students. Other schools choose professional books to read and discuss in "Book Club Groups" for their professional development. In this book, when we talk about "Book Club Groups," we mean that a teacher selects several books tied together by an author, comprehension strategy to be taught, or a theme or topic that is being studied. Usually, but not always, the four books selected are on different reading levels, and the class reads the books in their "Book Club Groups" and follows up the reading with group discussions or activities. Comprehension is always the focus of both the reading and the discussion.

How is this different from most reading groups? The difference is that the teacher has all of the groups in the class reading and responding to the different books they are reading at the same time during the Guided Reading portion of the school day. When using this during-reading format, a teacher does not have to worry about how to keep the rest of the children meaningfully occupied when she is working with just one reading group. In addition, because the books are tied together in a meaningful way, whole-class discussion can occur with applications for all of the students, regardless of their reading levels.

What Is Guided Reading?

Guided Reading has a long history and is not limited to leveled readers and leveled groups. *The Literacy Dictionary* (Harris and Hodges, 1995) defines Guided Reading like this:

". . . reading instruction in which the teacher provides the structure and purpose for reading and for responding to the material read. Note: Most basal reading programs have Guided Reading lessons."

A good Guided Reading lesson always has three phases: before-, during-, and after-reading. In Four-Blocks® classrooms, teachers use a variety of before- and after-reading formats depending on the material that is being read and the comprehension strategy that is being taught. Comprehension is always the focus of the Guided Reading lessons in Four-Blocks classrooms. (Cunningham, Hall, and Cunningham, 2000).

Four-Blocks teachers also use a variety of during-reading formats: echo reading, choral reading, shared reading, partner reading, small flexible groups, Three-Ring Circus, ERT, and the most multilevel format of all—Book Club Groups. The during-reading format that is chosen depends on the class, the students' reading levels, and the material they will read. As children become better and more independent readers, we like to use Book Club Groups more often. We also let children have some choice about what they read. In this book, we will describe some of the special features of Book Club Groups and then give some examples of lessons for Book Club Groups in first, second, and third grades.

What Are Book Club Groups?

For Book Club Groups, the teacher usually selects four books tied together by an author, theme, or topic. Hopefully, the books are on three or four different reading levels. The class is divided into four heterogeneous reading groups, and each group reads and discusses one of the four books, first in the group and then with the whole class. A teacher can use Book Club Groups to make connections to science and social studies, and to teach comprehension skills. The teacher can also select several books as part of an author study (Tomie dePaola, Arnold Lobel, Patricia Polacco, etc.), a book character study (Arthur, Miss Frizzle, Henry and Mudge, etc.), a genre study (biographies, mysteries, folktales, etc.), a reading skill focus (prediction, making connections, summarize, etc.), a social studies theme (families, transportation, communities, etc.), or a science theme (dinosaurs, plants, insects, etc.), or Book Club Groups can follow a whole-class reading of a book or genre, or the strategy can be done on its own.

In Four-Blocks classrooms, Book Club Groups offers a teacher and class a chance to read and discuss several different books on several different reading levels at the same time. The teacher's role is to circulate and see that all students are actively engaged with their groups, either reading or working on the after-reading activity. Sometimes the teacher chooses to let three groups operate independently because each Book Club Group has a leader and the teacher has taught the expected behaviors and procedures. The teacher sits down with one group and gives this group more guidance

[Introduction]

because those students need more help with the assigned task.

Sometimes the whole class reads a story in the basal reader or a whole-group set—maybe a story written by a well-liked author like Kevin Henkes—and the teacher follows the whole-class reading with Book Club Groups. The teacher usually selects four books by the author of the whole-class reading, keeping in mind the reading levels of students in the class. Following a book talk or an introduction to each of the four books by the same author, children preview the four selections and make their choices. While previewing the books, each student is asked to find a book she wants to read that is also a book she can read. So, glancing through the books and reading a page or two from each of the four choices is important on this day. After reading and discussing the books with the children in their groups, each child then lists which books she would like to read, indicating first, second, and third choices. Next, the teacher looks at students' choices and assigns them to their Book Club Groups.

The next day, each group will get to read one book. While the basal-reader selection or whole-group set was grade-level appropriate and focused on a skill that the students in that grade level need to learn, the books chosen for Book Club Groups are four different books on different reading levels—levels at which most of the class can read. Hopefully, one book is above grade level but within the levels of the best readers in the class. Another book is easier, but the struggling readers can read it with support. The two remaining books are average for the class, and many of the students can read these

books. Each Book Club Group is often on what teachers call, "the child's reading level."

Sometimes, it is not the readability level that makes a book more difficult or easy to read, but the content of the books and background knowledge of the students in the class. Suppose there are four different books on animals. Children may know a lot about the dogs, cats, and horses in three of the books because they know something about these animals. This makes those books easier selections than the other book about sea turtles. Background knowledge, how much is known about the subject of the text, makes books harder or easier for children to read.

Book Club Groups can include books from one genre—maybe all of the students read and discuss a mystery together, then follow that mystery with four more mysteries written on a variety of levels. At other times, teachers can use Book Club Groups when studying a theme or topic—animals, insects, families, or winter—so that all children have the opportunity to read something "just right" for them while learning about something new. However, in this era of accountability, teachers also need to do grade-level work if they plan to hold children accountable for grade-level standards and test them on grade-level materials. It only makes sense that students will not pass a test on material they have not been introduced to all year long. So, if students are to pass the grade-level tests, helping them master grade-level skills is as important as having materials that are "just right" for them to read. Yes, teaching young children to read is more complicated than some people make it seem!

Book Club Groups Procedure

As mentioned previously, the first day of Book Club Groups is usually spent previewing the books. The teacher might give the class a short book talk on each book, sharing the pictures as he talks. Or, the teacher might show the cover of each book and tell a little about the book—the characters, setting, etc. The teacher might also preview the books by looking at the pictures and discussing what students see happening in each book or reading aloud several pages of each book to students. After previewing, the teacher lets children spend a few minutes with each of the four books reading and thinking, "Is this a book I want to read? Is this a book I can read?" Finally, during the after-reading activity, each child in the class will indicate their first, second, and third choices for books they would like to read with a Book Club Group.

Whenever possible, in choosing the books for Book Club Groups, we try to include one that is easier and one that is harder. (We don't tell the children that some books are harder and easier!) If a child who is struggling chooses the easier book as one of her choices, she is put in the group that will read this book. If the more advanced readers choose the harder book for any of their choices, they are put in that group. Each time we do Book Club Groups, the groups change. While we do consider the reading levels and choices of children when assigning, the groups all have a range of readers and are not ability groups, but many children are reading books that are "just right" for them.

Once Book Club Groups are formed, the groups meet regularly to read and discuss their books. Book Club Groups can last from two days to two weeks or more if the class is reading novels.

The teacher rotates through the groups giving guidance, support, and encouragement. Each day, the groups report to the whole class what has happened or what they have learned from reading their books so far.

An Example: Dr. Seuss Book Club Groups

Here is an example of Book Club Groups that most teachers in grades one, two, and three can do with their classes. If teachers don't have several copies of four Dr. Seuss favorites, they can still use this strategy at little or no expense to them or their schools by asking children to bring in copies of Dr. Seuss books they have at home. For many classrooms, this is a good, easy way to begin Book Club Groups. Many teachers find this to be a fun activity in March as schools all over the United States are celebrating Dr. Seuss's birthday. First graders can read these books late in the year, mainly because so many are familiar with the books and have been for years. Second and third graders love to read and reread their favorite Dr. Seuss books.

Teachers often build up to this activity by reading Dr. Seuss books during the teacher read-aloud each day. Then, teachers encourage children to bring in copies of their favorite Dr. Seuss books from home. When children bring their favorite Dr. Seuss books to school, the teacher will notice there are often many copies of several books. The teacher can "borrow" these books from the children, combine them with library and classroom copies, and use them for Book Club Groups.

The Dr. Seuss books we have chosen for Book Club Groups are: *Hop on Pop* (Random House, 1963), *The Foot Book* (Random House, 1988),

One Fish Two Fish Red Fish Blue Fish (Random House, 1981) and *There's a Wocket in My Pocket* (Random House, 1974). (There were many others we could have chosen; so if you have favorites make substitutions.)

Dr. Seuss books are divided into two categories: The first is Beginner Books in which he uses words and pictures to encourage children to read all by themselves. The second category is Bright and Early Books in which the stories are brief and funny, while the words are few, easy, and have a happy, catchy rhythm. The pictures in the Bright and Early books offer clear and colorful clues to the text.

For our Book Club Groups, *Hop on Pop* is an easy selection because most of the pages have just two words with the same spelling pattern, and then a simple sentence or two using those two words (for example, "PUP CUP Pup in cup"). The pictures support the text and can be used by children to cross-check their reading and see if they have read it right by looking at the pictures and print. *The Foot Book* is also an easy selection in which the pictures and print support each other and are about different kinds of feet (for example, "Small feet big feet here come pig feet."). *One Fish Two Fish Red Fish Blue Fish* is more difficult than *Hop on Pop* or *The Foot Book* but can easily be read by many first- or second-grade children. There is more text on the pages in this book, but if students know their color and number words and if they understand rhyming words, they will be able to read this text that plays with words and introduces them to many funny things. (When you do Book Club Groups you usually want a book that is also a little more challenging than grade level for those who need that challenge.) For many children, the hardest of the four books may be *There's a Wocket in My Pocket* because there are many nonsense words ("wocket," "nureau," etc.) that have no real meaning. Dr. Seuss would say that we have chosen two Beginner Books and two Bright and Early Books.

Thus, we have four books with a range of beginning reading levels for our Book Club Groups. But, we do not put children in their groups solely by their reading abilities; children should have some choice as to which books they would like to read. Book Club Groups usually last for several days. The teacher decides that the Dr. Seuss Book Club Groups will last three days.

Suggested Books for the Dr. Seuss Book Club Groups (choose four):
- *The Cat in the Hat* (Random House, 1985) Beginner Books
- *The Foot Book* (Random House, 1988) Bright and Early Books
- *Green Eggs and Ham* (Random House, 1988) Beginner Books
- *Hop on Pop* (Random House, 1963) Beginner Books
- *I Can Read with My Eyes Shut!* (Random House, 1978) Beginner Books
- *Marvin K. Mooney Will You Please Go Now!* (Random House, 1972) Bright and Early Books
- *One Fish Two Fish Red Fish Blue Fish* (Random House, 1981) Beginner Books
- *Ten Apples Up On Top* (Theo. LeSieg, Random House, 1961) Bright and Early Books
- *There's a Wocket in My Pocket* (Random House, 1974) Beginner Books
- Any other Dr. Seuss books the teacher or the children have several copies of

[Introduction]

Day 1

Before:	Preview the four books with the class.
During:	Have each child look at and read a page or two from each of the four books.
After:	Have children select the books they want to read and write those choices on index cards.

The teacher begins the Guided Reading time by telling the children that she has selected four wonderful Dr. Seuss books for them to read in Book Club Groups. If this is the first session using this format, the teacher may talk about how grown-ups often read the same book and get together with friends to talk about the book. She might use Oprah's or some other book club as an example. Teachers who have read a selection with a Book Club Group may want to use this as an example for the children. (Both *Mosaic of Thought* by Ellin Keene and Susan Zimmerman and *Classrooms That Work* by Pat Cunningham and Dick Allington were discussed on *teachers.net* one year, and many schools used these two books for Book Club Groups as a part of their staff development.) The teacher then explains that the students are such good readers that they are now ready for Book Club Groups with their classmates and friends!

One at a time, the teacher shows the cover of each book and lets children tell what they know about the books and some of their personal experiences with these books. Using only the covers, she gets children thinking about what they know about these books and what they might read. Then, she tells children that they only have three days to spend on these books, and they don't have enough time or copies of the books for each child to read all four books. Each Book Club Group will read one book and hear about the other three books.

Next, the teacher hands each child an index card and asks him to write his name and the numerals one, two, and three on the card. The teacher explains that she will give students 20 minutes to preview the books—five minutes for each book. The teacher places all of the copies of each book in the four corners of the room. She randomly assigns the children to groups; the children in group one go to the first set of books, the children in group two go to the second set of books, the children in group three go to the third set of book, and the children in group four go to the fourth set of books. The teacher sets her timer for five minutes and tells the children that when the timer sounds, they must move to the next corner and the next group of books.

For the next 20 minutes, children are busy trying to read as much as they can and look at as many pages as they can. Every time the timer sounds and they have to move, some children groan. When the 20 minutes is up, children return to their seats to write down their first, second, and third choices on the index cards. It isn't easy! Most protest that they want to read them all! They have trouble deciding which are their first choices and which are their second choices. The teacher tells them not to worry too much about the order of choices because she can't guarantee they will get their first choices or even their second choices. She tells students,

"I want the groups to be about the same size, and I need to put groups together that will work well together. I promise I will give you one of your choices, and I will try to give you your first choices, but I can't promise that!"

After school, the teacher looks at all of the index cards. First, she looks at the cards of the struggling readers. Four of her five struggling readers have chosen *Hop on Pop* as one of their choices, so she puts them in the *Hop on Pop* group along with two more able readers who have also chosen *Hop on Pop*. (Why? As one excellent reader said, "*Hop on Pop* is a really funny book. It has always been my favorite Dr. Seuss book!") One struggling reader did not choose *Hop on Pop*, but he chose *The Foot Book* as his first choice, and the teacher puts him in *The Foot Book* group. Next, she looks at the choices of her most able readers. Four of them have chosen *There's A Wocket in My Pocket*, and she puts them in this group along with two fairly able readers. She puts the other eleven children in the remaining two groups, five in *The Foot Book* group and six in the *One Fish Two Fish Red Fish Blue Fish* group. The teacher also decides who will be the leader of each Book Club Group. Most children will be able to read their books independently; if they do have trouble, they can receive support from the leaders or classmates in their groups.

Day 2

Before:	Talk about the author of the books, Dr. Seuss, and tell children that they will read to the pages marked with paper clips and then talk about what they read.
During:	Have students echo read—the leader reads first and the other children in the group "echo" the reading by whispering. (If this is second or third grade, the group can read the whole book independently, or each member can take a turn and read a page.)
After:	Have children talk about what happened in their books with their groups. Then, choose a student from each group to report to the whole class.

The second day, the children read their books with their Book Club Groups. Before passing out the books, the teacher tells them how they will read, what their purpose is for reading, and what they will do after they read the books. The teacher explains that during reading today each group will echo read a book, as well as read and point. The children know that this means the leader will read each page first, while the others point to the words. Then, the rest of the group will try to be the echo—reading exactly the way the leader did. (Read and point is used in the early reading stages to help children stay focused and track print. If you teach second and third grade, you may want to have the children read these selections silently on both days.)

The children's purpose is to read the books with good expression, emphasizing the funny words and the rhyming words and to think about what they like best in their reading today. (What pictures do they like best? What words? What is really funny? What is really silly?) She explains that the groups will talk about these things after they read. If a group finishes before time is up, students should go back through the book and begin to talk about what they like best.

The teacher passes out the books. As she hands each group their books she says, "The one that gets the book with the index card in it is the leader today." She makes sure that a fluent reader and a responsible student is given that book.

As the children read, the teacher circulates, "drops an ear" and listens, coaches if needed, then moves on. She monitors most closely the *Hop on Pop* group, visiting them at the beginning and making sure they know what to do and how to do it. After she monitors the other groups, the teacher returns to the *Hop on Pop* group and coaches them some more, if needed.

As the groups finish reading, they begin to discuss what they liked about their books. They like the funny pictures, the rhyming words, and the silly things that Dr. Seuss writes about in his books. The leader of each group will share these things with the whole class in the after-reading phase of this lesson.

Day 3

Before:	Tell students they will finish reading (or reread) their books, and then talk about what was funny and what they liked about the books.
During:	Have students choral read—reading the pages together with the leader. (If this is second or third grade, the groups can read independently or each member can read a page.)
After:	Have children share the parts that are funny and the parts they like with their groups and with the whole class.

The third day, the children finish (or reread) their books with their Book Club Groups. This time, they will read the selections chorally. Their purpose is to find their favorite pages to read to the group. The teacher gives each child a bookmark. As they chorally read the pages, the children can put their bookmarks at their favorite pages. As each student continues and comes to an even "more favorite" page, he can move the bookmark. Once the whole book is read chorally, each child will practice reading his favorite page. The leader in each group makes sure each child can read the page fluently and can explain why it was chosen. If several children in a group have chosen the same page, they practice reading that page chorally. The Guided Reading block ends with all of the children reading aloud and explaining their choices. They talk about the pictures and what the author is saying on the page and how he illustrates the text. The teacher hears members of other groups saying, "I liked those funny fur feet, too!" or "The house on the mouse was the best illustration in that book, but a little mouse can't really carry a big house!" It is apparent from their faces and the talk that they want to read or reread these Dr. Seuss books again and again.

The teacher ends the lesson by telling the class that the Book Club Groups are over, but she wants to "borrow" these books a little longer. If the owners will let her, she will put one book from each group in each of the book baskets (or on the bookshelf) so that everyone has a chance to read or reread their favorite Dr. Seuss books at Self-Selected Reading time if they choose. The children are all anxious to read one or two books they did not get to read but wish they had.

Here are some other Book Club Groups we have seen teachers use successfully:

Book Club Groups—Author Studies
- David Adler (biographies)—second or third grade (Chapter 4, pages 122-129)
- Marc Brown (*Arthur*)—second grade (Chapter 2, pages 18-23)
- Eve Bunting—third grade (Chapter 2, pages 24-30)
- Joanna Cole (science: *The Magic School Bus*™ series)—third grade (Chapter 4, pages 174-182)
- Tomie dePaola—first or second grade (Chapter 2, pages 31-36)
- Gail Gibbons (science: animals)—late first, second, or third grade (Chapter 4, pages 147-155) (social studies: holidays)—first, second, or third grade (Chapter 4, pages 139-146)
- Kevin Henkes—first, second, or third grade (Chapter 2, pages 37-44)
- Arnold Lobel—late first or second grade (Chapter 2, pages 45-55)
- Laura Numeroff—late first or second grade (Chapter 2, pages 56-61)
- Peggy Parrish (*Amelia Bedelia*)—second or third grade (Chapter 2, pages 62-68)
- Patricia Polacco—third grade (Chapter 2, pages 69-75)
- Cynthia Rylant (*Henry and Mudge*)—second grade (Chapter 2, pages 76-82)
- Dr. Seuss—any grade level (Chapter 1, pages 9-14)

Book Club Groups to Teach Comprehension Strategies
- Make Text-to-Self Connections—second and third grade (Chapter 3, pages 93-100)
- Preview and Predict—second and third grade (Chapter 3, pages 85-92)
- Question and Monitor—second and third grade (Chapter 3, pages 101-107)
- Summarize and Conclude—first, second, and third grade (Chapter 3, pages 108-113)

Book Club Groups by Themes
Social Studies
- Biographies—late second or third grade (Chapter 4, pages 122-129)
- Families and Grandparents—first or second grade (Chapter 4, pages 116-121)
- Holidays—first, second, or third grade (Chapter 4, pages 139-146)
- Transportation—first or second grade (Chapter 4, pages 130-138)

Science
- Animals—late first, second, or third grade (Chapter 4, pages 147-155)
- Insects—late first, second, or third grade (Chapter 4, pages 164-173)
- Weather—late first, second, or third grade (Chapter 4, pages 156-163)

Reading Levels for the Books in *Book Club Groups*

The books listed for the Book Club Groups have been leveled for you. For most of the books, there will be a Guided Reading Level, or GRL, (Fountas and Pinnell) and a Reading Level, or RL, (Scholastic, Inc.). In some cases, one or both of these levels were unavailable. Books without a GRL or RL were leveled by the authors as Easy, Average, or Hard.

Book Club Groups by Author

One way to further children's interest in books and reading is to talk about the authors and illustrators of children's literature. Even the youngest children in school should be told the names of the authors who write their favorite stories and the books the teacher reads to the class. Publishers, newspapers, magazines, and the World Wide Web are sources of information about the authors of children's books. Some authors correspond to children through their publishers. Many authors have their own Web sites where children and teachers can find information about the authors and the books they have written.

Children's authors write about many different things. Some begin with a particular character or characters they write about. Before or during writing, authors must decide several things: What will this book be about? Who is the audience? What is the theme? What research needs to be done? Different authors write for different purposes. Some authors write to entertain, some to teach, and some to inform children about the world around them.

Many young children like Curious George, a mischievous monkey, because he is very curious and does all of the things they are not allowed to do. They wonder what will happen to him in each book. Children wonder the same thing with the popular book character, Arthur the aardvark, who is now a television star, too. Teachers can discuss a loose tooth, telling the truth, responsibility, a new baby, and other familiar topics after reading *Arthur* books. Kevin Henkes's mouse characters invite us to discuss individuality or friendship after reading some of his books.

When teachers read Patricia Polacco books, they know children will learn about families that may be alike or different from their families. They will hear about customs they may or may not be familiar with, also. Eve Bunting writes about "heavy" topics, such as homelessness, the Vietnam Memorial, learning to read as

"Children's authors write about many different things."

[Author]

an adult, and orphan trains. From her books, students can learn history, as well as tolerance and acceptance.

David Adler writes the easy-to-read *Cam Jansen* mysteries, as well as many easy-to-read picture biographies. Gail Gibbons helps children learn more about the world with books about animals, dinosaurs, berries, and holidays. Whatever children find fascinating, Gail Gibbons writes about.

There are hundreds of wonderful children's books, and for each age group there are several authors who seem to know what to say and how to say it so that young children can and will become readers. What follows are some popular children's authors for Book Club Groups and author studies for first-, second-, and third-grade classes. Some popular authors fall more nicely into social studies (David Adler and Gail Gibbons) or science (Gail Gibbons) categories. (There are other authors who are just as popular that we have not included, so do not feel limited by this list when selecting books for your students to read in Book Club Groups.)

Author: Marc Brown

Marc Brown has written over 25 books about Arthur, an aardvark, and his adventures with his family and friends. Brown's writing is clever and appealing to young children. He said that his grandmother told him the most wonderful stories while he was growing up in Pennsylvania. When he became a father, Brown began to tell stories to his first son before he went to sleep. One night, his story was about an aardvark that hated his nose. The aardvark became Arthur and the story became *Arthur's Nose* (Little, Brown and Co., 1979), the first book in the *Arthur* Adventure series. He has hidden the names of his sons, Tolon and Tucker, in all but one of the *Arthur* books. The name of his daughter, Eliza, appears in his newer books. Brown has also written a series of books based on D. W., Arthur's little sister. He now lives in Hingham, Massachusetts, and Martha's Vineyard with his wife (who is an illustrator and author) and their daughter, Eliza. *Arthur* now appears on a television series every day on PBS. *Arthur* books are just right for lots of second-grade children.

Suggested Marc Brown/*Arthur* Books for Book Club Groups (choose four):
- *Arthur Writes a Story* (Little, Brown and Co., 1996) GRL: K; RL: 2.4
- *Arthur's Computer Disaster* (Little, Brown and Co., 1997) GRL: L; RL: 2.2
- *Arthur's Pet Business* (Little, Brown and Co., 1997) GRL: K; RL: 2.5
- *Arthur's Teacher Trouble* (Little, Brown and Co., 1986) GRL: K; RL: 3.8
- *Arthur's Thanksgiving* (Scholastic, Inc., 1983) GRL: L; RL: 2.5
- *Arthur's Tooth* (Little, Brown and Co., 1985) GRL: K; RL: 2.5
- Any of the other *Arthur* Adventure books

[Marc Brown]

Purpose

To look at the four books and decide which book each student would like to read and can read while previewing the four possible Book Club Group selections

Before:	Model how to select a book.
During:	Have students review the four books, reading a page or two from each book.
After:	Let children discuss in their groups the books they liked, then discuss with the whole class. Finally, let the students list their book choices.

Preparation/Materials Needed

- A list of children randomly assigned to four groups
- Student copies (five to seven) of the four books to be previewed are placed in the four corners of the room, in baskets around the room, or at tables so that students can preview them—one title per corner, basket, or table.
- Index cards/pieces of paper and pencils/pens to write Book Club Group choices

Before Reading

Take students for a short "picture walk" (or "book talk") through the four books, talking about who is in this story, where the story takes place, and what is happening. Randomly assign children to one of four preview groups, and choose a leader for each of the four groups. Tell students, "Today, you will have a chance to preview the four books. Then, you will get to choose which book you would like to read for our Book Club Groups. Marc Brown is the author of all four of these *Arthur* books. You may like one or two of the books better than others. Your job today is to find a book you want to read—one that interests you. But, remember it must also be a book you can read—one where you already know most of the words." (You may need to teach the "five-finger rule"—more than five words missed on a page means the book will probably be too hard to read.)

During Reading

Explain the procedure to students by saying, "Today, you will move from table to table (from corner to corner, basket to basket, etc.) to preview each of the four Book Club Groups selections. You will have five minutes to preview each book. First, look at the pictures in the book to see what the book is about and whether it looks interesting. Next, read a page or two to see if you can read it. When the five minutes are up, I will give you a signal (set a timer for five minutes or use the classroom clock and ring a bell) and then you will move to the next set of books and preview that title. When you have previewed all four books, you are ready talk about the books with your group and then make your decision."

After Reading

Let students discuss the books they liked with their groups, then the class. Give each student an index card or piece of paper to list his first, second, and third choices. Then, have students give you the index cards so that you can make Book Club Group assignments.

[Marc Brown]

Purpose

To begin reading the books and find out about characters, setting, and what happened to Arthur in each book

Before:	Talk about the characters, setting, and what is happening to Arthur in each book.
During:	Tell students to read half of their books with their groups (echo, partner, taking turns reading a page each, or independent reading) and discuss the characters, setting, and Arthur's problems in their books with their groups.
After:	Let one student in each group share the characters, setting, and what is happening in the group's book.

Preparation/Materials Needed:

- Student copies (five to seven) of the chosen books
- Create and post the groups based on the students' choices.

Before Reading

Tell students, "Today, you will meet in your Book Club Groups for the first time." Talk about the Book Club Groups and how each group will read a different book to find out about the characters, setting, and what happened to Arthur in the books. Your picture walk (Day 1, page 19) and their preview of the books gave students some idea of what happened in each book. Now, each group will read their book and find out and discuss exactly what happened. Today, have students read half of the books and finish the stories tomorrow. Tell students to pay attention to the characters, the setting, and what is happening in their books. This is what they will talk about after reading.

During Reading

Instruct children to read half of their books. They will read to good stopping points in the stories, marked by paper clips you insert approximately halfway into the books, as there are no page numbers you can assign. Ask children to echo read with leaders (if the books seem hard for many students), partner read (if the books seem just about right for the class), take turns and read a page each, or read silently and independently (if the books can be read easily by most students). The during-reading strategy always depends on the grade level, the readability of the text, the reading level of most of the children in the class, and the time of year it is read. If reading out loud, each student in the group reads one or two pages, starting with the leader and going around the group clockwise. Unlike round robin reading, when working in small groups, all children will get to read that day. After reading, each group will discuss the characters, setting, and Arthur's problem in this book. During the reading and discussion, monitor the class by walking around the room, "dropping an ear" and listening, and coaching the groups that need help as they begin to read and discuss their books.

After Reading

After children have discussed the books in their groups, bring the class back to a large group setting and have a member of each group (it can be the leader or another student) share with the class the characters, setting, and the problem Arthur has in the book.

[Marc Brown]

Purpose

To read their books and talk about the conclusion of each

Before:	Tell children to finish their books and be ready to discuss how their books end.
During:	Have children finish reading their books, using the same during-reading strategy as Day 2 (echo reading, partner reading, taking turns reading a page each, or independent reading).
After:	Instruct each group to come up with a sentence or two about the conclusion of their book.

Preparation/Materials Needed

- Student copies (five to seven) of the chosen books
- Sheet of large chart paper and a dark-colored marker for each group to write a sentence about what happened to Arthur and the conclusion of their book

Before Reading

Tell students, "Today, after reading, your group will come up with a sentence or two that tells how your book end—the conclusion." Remind children of a time you have done this with the whole class after reading a book or story, or a time you modeled this in your Writing mini-lesson. Make sure to stress that when they write a sentence or two, they don't want to tell too much. They do not have to include everything they read, just enough so that everyone will know what happened to Arthur and the other characters in the book.

During Reading

Students will finish reading their books with their groups. Remind students of how they will read and that when they finish, the leaders will begin discussions of how the books ended. Monitor and coach the groups as they read. Help those groups that need help writing a sentence or two about how their stories ended. (To avoid this problem, choose a strong reader and writer as the leader in each group.)

After Reading

Bring the class back together in a large-group setting and let each group share their sentences about Arthur and the conclusion of their story.

[Marc Brown]

Extensions

Self-Selected Reading

- For your teacher read-aloud, read some of Marc Brown's other books; especially the first book *Arthur's Nose* in which Arthur looks more like an aardvark than the television personality we may recognize.
- Encourage children to read a book or books at Self-Selected Reading time that they did not read during Book Club Groups.

Writing

- Encourage students to use the information that their group gathered (characters, setting, what happened to Arthur, how did it end) to write book reviews of their book. Read some reviews from Sunday newspapers or magazines to help.
- Do an interactive writing mini-lesson and develop an Arthur story with your class. Then, let the children try it on their own.

Art

- Have each student draw a picture of what happened to Arthur and the main characters in her group's book.
- Direct students to draw pictures of their favorite parts of the stories.
- Make copies of the written directions (page 184) and make some Arthur chenille craft stick glasses with your class.

Working with Words

- Make up four sentences, one from each book, and use them for a Guess the Covered Word activity. Here is an example with the covered words in bold:

  1. When the computer crashed, Arthur looked for help from a **friend**.
  2. The best story that Arthur wrote was a **real** one.
  3. Arthur had not lost a tooth, but **Francine** had.
  4. When Arthur started a pet business, he cared for a **bird**.

- Do a Making Words lesson with the name **Arthur**.

  Letters: a, u, h, r, r, t
  Make: at hat rat/art (Art) rut hut hurt that Ruth Arthur
  Sort: beginning sounds—r, h; spelling patterns—-at, -ut
  Transfer: scat, brat, nut, shut

- Do a Making Words lesson with the word **computer**.

  Letters: e, o, u, c, m, p, t, r
  Make: up to top mop Tom pot rot tore more core rope come comet mope computer
  Sort: beginning sounds—m, c; spelling patterns—-op, -ot, -ore
  Transfer: stop, crop, spot, chore

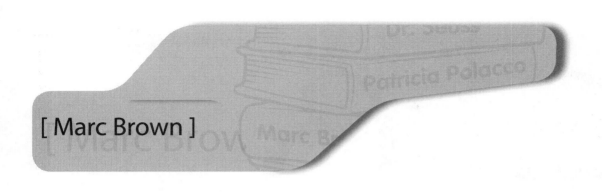

[Marc Brown]

- Do a Making Words lesson with the holiday **Thanksgiving**.

  Letters: a, i, i, g, g, h, k, n, n, s, t, v
  Make: an at it in tin tan/ant van vain gain sank tank thank Thanksgiving
  Sort: beginning sounds—t, th; spelling patterns—-an, -ank
  Transfer: plan, bran, blank, crank

- Do a Making Words lesson with the word **animals**.

  Letters: a, a, i, l, m, n, s
  Make: an am aim Sam slam mail nail sail snail nasal salami animals
  Sort: beginning sounds–s, n; spelling patterns—-am, -ail
  Transfer: jam, cram, jail, trail

Author: Eve Bunting

Eve Bunting has written more than 200 children's books. She presents young readers with a child's-eye view of complex individual, family, social, and historical issues. Some of these issues (homelessness, riots, etc.) are not pleasant to think and read about, but many young children often have to deal with or will observe these in their everyday lives. All of the books are written from a child's point of view. Bunting's books create many interesting connections, questions, comments, and discussions whether read aloud by the teacher, read by the whole class, or read in Book Club Groups. The topics, length, and readability of many of Bunting's books are more appropriate for third and fourth graders than younger readers. Eve Bunting now lives in Pasadena, California.

Suggested Eve Bunting Books for Book Club Groups (choose four):
- *Dandelions* (Voyager, 1995) GRL: N; RL: 3.1
- *A Day's Work* (Clarion Books, 1994) GRL: K; RL: 3.1
- *Fly Away Home* (Clarion Books, 1991) GRL: M; RL: 4.3
- *Going Home* (HarperTrophy, 1996) GRL: K; RL: 5.4
- *How Many Days to America?: A Thanksgiving Story* (Clarion Books, 1988) GRL: S; RL: 3.2
- *The Memory String* (Clarion Books, 2000) GRL: N; RL: 3.4
- *Our Teacher's Having a Baby* (Clarion Books, 1992) GRL: M; RL: 3.9
- *Smoky Night* (Voyager, 1994) GRL: P; RL: 2.5
- *Train to Somewhere* (Clarion Books, 1996) GRL: Q; RL: 2.8
- *The Wall* (Clarion Books, 1990) GRL: N; RL: 3.1
- *The Wednesday Surprise* (Clarion Books, 1989) GRL: K; RL: 2.9

[Eve Bunting]

Purpose

For students to make predictions about the four books and decide what books they would like to read while previewing the four Book Club Group selections

Before:	Model how you select a book.
During:	Have students preview the four books, reading a page or two from each of them.
After:	Ask students to list their book choices and discuss questions they had with their groups, then the class.

Preparation/Materials Needed

- A list of children randomly assigned to four groups
- Student copies (five to seven) of the four books to be previewed are placed in the four corners of the room, in baskets around the room, or at tables so that students can preview them—one title per corner, basket, or table.
- Index cards/pieces of paper and pencils/pens to write Book Club Group choices

Before Reading

Tell students, "Today, you will have a chance to preview the books you will get to choose from for your Book Club Groups. Eve Bunting is the author of all four books. You may like one or two of the books better than others. Your job today is to find a book you want to read–one that interests you. But, remember it must also be a book you can read—one where you already know most of the words. (You may need to teach the "five-finger rule"—more than five words missed on a page means the book will probably be too hard to read.) Good readers often ask themselves questions while they look at or preview books. The questions they ask often create a desire to read the books in order to answer those questions and to satisfy their curiosity. This may happen to you today when you are previewing these books."

Pick up a copy of one of the picture books you have personally selected and say, "I'd like to model for you how I select a book. I selected this book from the bookstore (or library) a while ago. When I first saw this book and looked at the cover, it caught my interest right away. After a moment or two, I opened the book, started to look at some of the pictures, and before I knew it, I had asked myself some questions that I wanted answered. Let me show you how it happened." Continue by describing what you predicted the book would be about and a question or two you had about the book in your hand. Make sure you explain why the prediction and/or questions helped you make the decision to read the book.

Finally, tell students, "Today, you will get a chance to spend some time with each of these four books. Look at the title, and pictures, and think about what you want to know and what you think the book will be about based on what you see."

During Reading

Assign students randomly to four groups and choose a leader for each group. Tell the class, "Today, you will move from table to table (from corner to corner, basket to basket, etc.) to

[Eve Bunting]

preview each of our Book Club Group selections. You will have five minutes to preview each book. First, look at the pictures to see what the book is about and whether it looks interesting. Next, see if you can read it. When three minutes are up, I will tell you, and you will have two more minutes to write a question you have about the book. Then, you will move to another table (basket, corner, etc.). You will do this four times until you have visited the four tables (baskets, corners, etc.) and previewed all four books."

After Reading

Have students turn over their index cards and write the titles of the three books they would like to read. The titles should be numbered 1, 2, and 3 to indicate their first, second, and third choices. Allow students time in their groups to discuss why they made their choices and talk about some questions they had about these books with other members of their groups.

Purpose

For students to begin to read the books to find answers to the questions they had when previewing

Before:	Talk about Book Club Group questions and how students will read and find the answers to the questions they asked when previewing the books.
During:	In groups, have each child read aloud one page of the group's book. Students talk about any answers to the questions that were found as they read the selection.
After:	Let each group share with the class questions they had and answers they found.

Preparation/Materials Needed

- Student copies (five to seven) of the chosen books
- Create and post a list of the groups based on students' choices.
- Create a student "Book Club Preview Questions" chart using some interesting questions from students' cards (at least one from each book).

Before Reading

Begin by telling students, "Today, you will meet in your Book Clubs Groups for the first time. Your first job will be to share questions you developed while previewing this book yesterday. Then, you will begin to read the book. I have used a paper clip to mark the page in each book where you should stop reading today. After reading, you need to tell your group the answers

[Eve Bunting]

to any questions you had when previewing the book yesterday."

During Reading

Let students know the format for reading, "Today in your Book Club Groups, you will each read a page out loud starting with the leader. After you finish reading the selection, you can talk about any questions that were answered and be ready to share them with the whole class." If having each student reading a page to the group seems too hard for most students, then let them partner read or echo read (leader reads each page line-by-line, pausing to let the group repeat, or echo, each line). Leaders should

be good readers who can easily read the pages and be good models for the other children in the groups. Monitor and coach the groups as they read, and answer or add questions.

After Reading

Bring the class back together in a large-group setting and discuss one or more of the interesting questions and answers from each group. Each group will be asked to supply possible answers to some of the questions they had yesterday that you recorded on the group chart. As each group gives an answer, write it below the question on the chart using a different-colored marker.

Purpose

For students to finish their books and complete summary statements

Before:	Talk about a summary.
During:	Have children finish reading their books with the groups, using the same during-reading format as yesterday (taking turns reading a page out loud, partner reading, or echo reading).
After:	Tell each group to come up with a summary of their book and share the summary with the class.

Preparation/Materials Needed

• Student copies (five to seven) of the chosen books
• Large sheet of chart paper and a dark-colored marker for each group to write a summary statement

Before Reading

Tell students, "Today, after reading, each group will create a sentence or two that tells what the book you read is about." Remind children of a time when you have summarized with the whole class after reading a book or story, or a time when you modeled summary in your Writing mini-lesson. Make sure to stress that when you write a summary they don't want to tell too

[Eve Bunting]

much, just enough so that everyone will know about the book. They do not have to include all of the details.

During Reading
Instruct students to finish reading their books by taking turns reading pages to the group. Monitor and coach the groups.

After Reading
Have each group complete a summary of their book. Help those groups that need help writing good summaries, or avoid this problem by choosing group leaders who are strong readers and writers. Bring the class back together in a large-group setting and let each group share their completed book summary with the whole class.

[Eve Bunting]

Extensions

Self-Selected Reading

- Encourage children to read other books by Eve Bunting during Self-Selected Reading, especially the ones that they did not read during Book Club Groups.

- If it is December, *Night Tree* (Voyager Books, 1991) is a good story for a read–aloud. It is about a family that makes an annual Christmastime visit to the woods to decorate an evergreen tree with food for the forest animals. *Night Tree* is not as "heavy" as most of Bunting's other books.

- *Going Home* (HarperTrophy, 1996) is another holiday story. This time, Bunting tells about a Mexican family that comes to the United States to work as farm laborers but still consider Mexico to be home. Christmas is coming, and Carlos and his family are going to Mexico. It is there that he realizes home is where people love you.

Writing

- During your Writing mini-lesson, write a summary of another Eve Bunting book with your students. If you have read the book aloud to your students, you can do interactive writing with your students helping you compose as you write.

- Have children write letters to Eve Bunting telling her about the books they read and why they liked them.

Guided Reading

- Be sure to let the children ask questions about selections they will read before they read the selections and then answer the questions after reading.

- Writing a summary of something the students have read is always a good after–reading strategy whether it is done independently, as a group, or a shared writing with the class.

Working with Words

- Do a Making Words lesson with the word **dandelions**.

  Letters: a, e, i, o, d, d, l, n, n, s
  Make: an Dan and Nan sand land lane line lions lanes alone dandelions
  Sort: names, plurals, spelling patterns— -an, -and
  Transfer: plans, grand, brand, brands

- Do a Making Words lesson with the word **grandfather**.

  Letters: a, a, e, d, f, g, h, n, r, r, t
  Make: an ran fan fat hat and hand head grand father grandfather
  Sort: spelling patterns—-an, -at, -and
  Transfer: plan, that, band, brand

- Do a Making Words lesson with the word **grandmother**.

  Letters: a, e, o, d, g, h, m, n, r, r, t
  Make: an ran man mat hat and hand head grand mother grandmother
  Sort: spelling patterns—-an, -at, -and
  Transfer: bran, van, scat, land

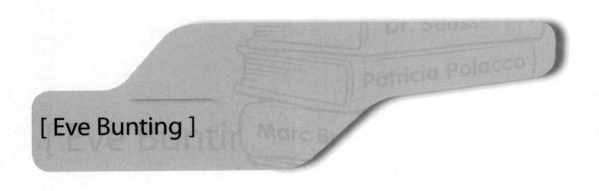

[Eve Bunting]

- Do a Making Words lesson with the word **family**.

    Letters: a, i, f, l, m, y

    Make: if my may/yam Fay fly aim ail fail mail film filmy family

    Sort: beginning sounds—f, m; spelling patterns—-y (i), -y (e), -ay, -ail, -aim

    Transfer: tray, stray, claim, snail

[Tomie dePaola]

"We met Tommy when I read the book *The Art Lesson* to you during a read-aloud one day. The entire story was about Tommy. Tommy is what we call the main character. On the Story Map beside 'Character(s)' write 'Tommy.' Today, as you read your stories again, think about who the main characters are in your stories. Each group has ten self-stick notes to write the actions, thoughts, and feelings of their main characters. Start by reading your story, stopping occasionally to record any new information you have about the main character(s). If you finish early, you may create a drawing of your character(s) on chart paper."

During Reading

Ask students to reread their books with partners or independently (silent reading) in their groups. Explain, "Today, your groups will start by rereading the stories. Stop occasionally as you read to record on the self-stick notes anything you learn about the main characters, setting, or what is happening in the book. When you are finished, you will discuss what you learned from your reading and be ready, as a group, to discuss the main character(s) in your book." Monitor each of the four groups as children read the stories and write on self-stick notes the things that they learn about their characters.

After Reading

Have the groups use the information from their self-stick notes to complete their group's Story Maps. Then, call the groups together again and have one student from each group show the picture (if her group started one) and talk about the main character and any other important characters in the group's book. If you have time, compare these books and characters by Tomie dePaola. Were any of the characters the same? Were any of the characters alike? What about the stories—alike or different? What was alike? What was different?

[Tomie dePaola]

Extensions

Self-Selected Reading

- Read aloud to the class more Tomie dePaola books, including the chapter books in the *26 Fairmount Avenue* series (Putnam Publishing Group), or some of his other books that students have not heard, which may include *Strega Nona* titles, other legends and folktales, *The Popcorn Book* (Holiday House, 1984), and *Meet the Barkers: Morgan and Moffat Go to School.*
- Encourage students to read the books their group did not read. This may mean that you need to take a trip to the school library/media center or the local library. Place lots of Tomie dePaola books on your classroom library shelves or in you Self-Selected Reading book baskets.

Writing

- Have each child write a summary of the character(s) she read about in her group's book.
- Have children compare two of Tomie dePaola's characters or books using Venn diagrams or "double bubbles."
- The children can write to Tomie dePaola.

Working with Words

Choose some of the names from Tomie dePaola's books for some "Making Names" lessons, which are done just like Making Words lessons. (*Making Names* by Pat Cunningham, Carson-Dellosa, 2004).

- Do a Making Names lesson with the name **Anthony**.
  Letters: a, o, h, n, n, t, y
  Make: an at on hay tan/ant Nan hat Tony than annoy Anthony
  Sort: beginning sounds—h; spelling patterns—-an, -at; names
  Transfer: scat, splat, plan, van
- Do a Making Words lesson with the word **bluebonnet**.
  Letters: e, e, o, u, b, b, l, n, n, t
  Make: be on lot not net beet blue teen tone bone bonnet bluebonnet
  Sort: beginning sounds—b, bl; spelling patterns—-ot, -one
  Transfer: spot, trot, cone, phone

Author: Kevin Henkes

Kevin Henkes is another wonderful, popular children's author. He uses animals, many times mice, as characters in his books. These animal characters experience similar problems and situations as humans. Most children really relate to Henkes's characters and draw parallels to their own lives. Kevin Henkes's language and humor are understandable, believable, and funny for young and older readers alike. We feel like we have met his characters before, but they were people, not animals, with the same problems! His books, especially *Chrysanthemum*, have become favorites of school children in primary grades in the past decade.

Suggested Kevin Henkes Books for Book Club Groups (choose four):
- *Chester's Way* (Greenwillow Books, 1988) GRL: K; RL: 3.1
- *Jessica* (Greenwillow Books, 1989) GRL: K; RL: 1.9
- *Julius: The Baby of the World* (Greenwillow Books, 1990) GRL: K; RL: 2.9
- *Lilly's Purple Plastic Purse* (Greenwillow Books, 1996) GRL: M; RL: 3.5
- *Owen* (Greenwillow Books, 1993) GRL: K; RL: 2.5
- *Sheila Rae, the Brave* (Mulberry Books, 1996) GRL: K; RL: 2.3
- *A Weekend with Wendell* (Mulberry Books, 1995) GRL: K; RL: 3.1
- *Wemberly Worried* (Greenwillow Books, 2000) GRL: H; RL: 2.1

Whole-Class Book for Day 1:
- *Chrysanthemum* (Greenwillow Books, 1991) GRL: L; RL: 4.2
  This book is about a little mouse that loves her name until she goes to school and is made fun of by her classmates. Then, Chrysanthemum loses confidence until her music teacher helps her realize how special her name really is.

[Kevin Henkes]

Purpose

For students to identify the characters, setting, and problem in the story and suggest three solutions; then, to identify the solution from a text

Before:	Discuss how a character's problems are often used for the plot (action) of a story and how it helps us to make connections to the story. Read to find Chrysanthemum's problem.
During:	First grade—Teacher reads aloud while students follow along in text. Second and third grades—Partner reading or independent reading
After:	Discuss how Chrysanthemum solved her problem and share connections to text.

Preparation/Materials Needed

- Copies of *Chrysanthemum* by Kevin Henkes for you and class
- Chart paper and markers
- Problem and Solution Chart written on chart paper (page 186)
- Optional: Internet connected to the author's Web site at *www.kevinhenkes.com*

Before Reading

On this first day, discuss how an author often uses a character's problems to set the plot (action) of the text. Discuss how identifying the problem can help the reader make a connection to the text and comprehend (understand) the text better. Tell students, "Today, we are going to read a book by Kevin Henkes. In this book the character has a problem. We are going to find the problem and discuss some solutions for the problem." Display the cover of the book. Ask students if they have read any other books by Kevin Henkes. Go to *www.kevinhenkes.com* and read the page about how Kevin began writing (*www.kevinhenkes.com/meet/kevin.asp*). Show students the Problems and Solution Chart (page 186). Answer any questions they may have about the form or the plan for reading.

During Reading

Read *Chrysanthemum* aloud and have students follow along in their texts, stopping when the problem of the story is evident. (If you teach second grade, students may read with partners. Third-grade students might read independently.) Ask students, "What do you think Chrysanthemum's problem is? Who can read the sentences in the book that helped you figure out her problem? Who can read that sentence aloud for me? How can Chrysanthemum solve her problem?" (Give students time to look for the answer then call on a student to read the sentences.) Write the problem and the suggested solutions from the students' forms on a large piece of chart paper or a transparency. Have students elaborate on their thoughts by asking questions, such as "Why do you think that?" or "What clues from the story let you know that?" This will help students justify their thinking. Accept all possible answers, praising those students who elaborate with or without prompting. Decide as a group which problem to list on the chart and do so. Read a little further in the story and talk about how the problem continues to trouble Chrysanthemum. "Who can read the sentences that tell us that Chrysanthemum is still worried

[Kevin Henkes]

about her name?" (Let the children find them and ask someone to read those sentences.) Ask students what steps Chrysanthemum's parents take to help make her feel better. (Then, let students locate that information in the text and ask someone to read those lines aloud.) Finally, ask students to suggest ways Chrysanthemum can solve her problem. List their suggestions on the chart.

After Reading

Discuss with the class how Chrysanthemum's problem was solved and other solutions to the problem. Allow children time to share connections they made to the text. (Did this ever happen to them or family members or friends?)

Extension—Character Education

If time permits, discuss the character education issues of acceptance and tolerance. Help students realize how their words might hurt others. One way to do this is to cut out a heart shape from pink or red construction paper. Have students sit in a circle and pass the heart around as they mimic the hurtful things the characters in the story said to Chrysanthemum. As each student makes a comment, have her crinkle a part of the paper heart. When the heart makes it back to you, begin passing it again, having each student say he is sorry and smooth out part of the heart. When the heart returns to you again, discuss how the heart looks different than it did before the activity began. Tell children that words hurt, and even if people say they are sorry, they can never take back the damage their words do to others.

[Kevin Henkes]

Purpose

To give a short book talk about the four selected Kevin Henkes's books and to model for students how to decide what book they would like to read while previewing the four possible Book Club Group texts

Before:	Give book talks and model how to select a book.
During:	Have students preview the four selected books, reading a page or two from each.
After:	Ask students to list book choices and discuss the books they liked with their groups and then with the class.

Preparation/Materials Needed

- A list of children randomly assigned to four groups
- Student copies (five to seven) of the four books to be previewed are placed in the four corners of the room, in baskets around the room, or at tables so that students can preview them—one title per corner, basket, or table.
- Index cards/pieces of paper and pencils/pens to write Book Club Group choices

Before Reading

Tell students, "Today, each of you will have a chance to preview four books, and then you will get to choose which one you would like to read with a Book Club Group. Kevin Henkes, one of my favorite authors, wrote and illustrated all four books. One of the books, I have read to you before. I will do a short picture walk through each of the four books, talking about the characters and what is happening. (Do this now using each of the four books you have chosen for your class to read.) Next, you will preview all four of the books and get to choose your first, second, and third choices for your Book Club Groups. You may like one or two of the Kevin Henkes's books better than the other books, or you may like them all—like me! Your job today is to find a book you want to read—one that interests you. But, remember it must also be a book you can read—one where most of the words you know. (If you have taught the five-finger rule, then remind students of it. See page 19.) So, as you look through each book with your groups today, be thinking, 'Is this a book I want to read and a book that I can read?'"

During Reading

Assign students to the four groups you randomly selected before the lesson, then choose a leader for each group. Tell students, "Today, you will move from table to table (corner to corner, basket to basket, etc.) to preview each of our Book Club Group selections. You will have five minutes to preview each book. First, look at the pictures to see what the book is about and if it looks interesting. Next, see if you can read it. When the three minutes are up, I will tell you. Then, you will have two more minutes to write a question you have about the book. Finally, you will move to another table (corner, basket, etc.). You will do this four times until you have visited the four tables (corners, baskets, etc.) and previewed all four books."

[Kevin Henkes]

After Reading

Have students turn over their question cards and write the numbers 1, 2, and 3. The titles of the books they would like to read should be written beside the numbers 1, 2, and 3 to indicate their first, second, and third choices. Allow students time in their groups to discuss why they made their choices and talk about some questions they had about these books with other members of their groups.

Purpose

For students to talk about Kevin Henkes's style and read the four books to find characters, setting, and a problem in each book

Before:	Talk about the characters, setting, and the problem in each book.
During:	Have children read their books to their group. After each group finishes their book, have them talk about the problem in their book.
After:	Let one student in each group share with the class the characters, setting, and problem in the group's book.

Preparation/Materials Needed:

- Student copies (five to seven) of the chosen books
- Chart paper for each group to record characters, setting, and problem
- Crayons, markers, or colorful pencils for each group

- Create and post a list of the groups based on the choices students wrote on their cards; indicate group leaders by marking with asterisks or highlighting.

Before Reading

Review the story of *Chrysanthemum* with students. (See pages 38-39.) Show the covers of the two books chosen for Book Club Groups to the students. Ask them if they can use what they know about Henkes's style (the way he writes) in *Chrysanthemum* to predict what may happen in each of the other books. List the students' predictions on chart paper. Each group should read the story and locate the problem in their book. Once students know the problem, they should list three possible solutions for that problem.

During Reading

Have students work together in their groups (echo reading, partner reading, or reading by themselves, depending on the grade level and reading levels of students in your class) to read the selected books. While reading, group members should identify the problem in

[Kevin Henkes]

their book. Finally, each group should discuss the problem and come up with three possible solutions. Monitor and coach the four groups, or a group that may need extra help, noting and praising students as they identify problems and come up with good solutions.

After Reading

Meet back as a whole class to discuss the problems each character has in the four chosen books. Read each group's list of possible solutions to their problem.

Purpose:

For students to identify the solution to the problem in each of Henkes's books

Before:	Talk about how each group will read their book and find the solution to the problem in their book today.
During:	Have students reread their books with partners in their groups and then talk about the solution.
After:	Let a student from each group report to the whole class the solution to the problem.

Preparation/Materials Needed:

- Create and post the Book Club Groups; assign leaders to each group.
- Student copies (five to seven) of the chosen books
- A piece of chart paper for each group to recorded the problems and solutions
- Crayons, markers, or colorful pencils for each group

Before Reading

Review the problem from each story. Discuss the purpose for reading—to find the solution. Tell students that after they finish reading, they will compare the characters, problems, and solutions from the stories they are reading to those in *Chrysanthemum*.

[Kevin Henkes]

During Reading

Send students to groups to read (echo reading, partner reading, or independent silent reading). Then, have each group, led by a leader, complete the chart by writing the problem, possible solutions, and the solution from the book. While the groups are reading, monitor and coach them, helping students to find the right information for their charts and showing students how to record information on the charts comparing the four Book Club Group choices with *Chrysanthemum*.

After Reading

Get the whole class back together and allow time for each group to share their chart with the class as you (or a student) write their response on a class comparison chart. All of the groups will come to the circle and share their information with the other groups, discussing how their book is alike and different from the other Kevin Henkes's books.

Extensions

Self-Selected Reading

- Read aloud some of Kevin Henkes's other books.
- Make a variety of Kevin Henkes's books available for students to choose to read during Self-Selected Reading time.

Writing

- Encourage each student to write about a problem he might have had with a friend and explain how he solved his problem.
- Let students write to Kevin Henkes telling him which books they have read, which books they like, and why they enjoy his books.

Guided Reading

- Make the class Book Club Group story form with three possible solutions available to students as they read other Kevin Henkes's texts.
- Toss a beach ball with story questions on it (Who were the characters? What was the setting? What happened at the beginning? Middle? End?) Have children answer the story questions after reading a Kevin Henkes's story and find the solutions in the book.

[Kevin Henkes]

Working with Words

Use some words or names from Kevin Henkes's books for Making Words lessons.

- Do a Making Words lesson with the name, **Chrysanthemum**.

    Letters: a, e, u, c, h, h, m, m, n, r, s, t, y
    Make: us as an ant/tan can the hen hem them then came same name anthem Chrysanthemum
    Sort: beginning sounds—th; spelling patterns—-an, -em, -en, -ame
    Transfer: plan, gem, pen, flame

- Do a Making Words lesson with the word, **friends**.

    Letters: e, i, d, f, n, r, s
    Make: if is rid red end ends/send/dens Fred fires/fries friends
    Sort: beginning sounds—s, d, fr; spelling patterns—-ed, -end; plurals
    Transfer: bled, sped, spend, blend

Author: Arnold Lobel

Arnold Lobel is a well-loved children's author. He is most famous for his *Frog and Toad* stories. He was one of the first children's authors to begin writing easy chapter books for young children. Through his two lovable characters, Frog and Toad, children learn valuable lessons about friendship and find that they, too, can read chapter books—a new milestone for many first and second graders.

Suggested Arnold Lobel Books for Book Club Groups (choose four):
- *Days with Frog and Toad* (HarperTrophy, 1984) GRL: J; RL: 2.1
- *Frog and Toad All Year* (HarperTrophy, 1984) GRL: K; RL: 2.2
- *Frog and Toad Together* (HarperTrophy, 1979) GRL: K; RL: 2.3
- *Grasshopper on the Road* (HarperTrophy, 1986) GRL: L; RL: 2.4
- *Mouse Soup* (HarperCollins, 1977) GRL: J; RL: 2.2
- *Mouse Tales* (HarperCollins, 1972) GRL: J; RL: 2.6
- *Owl at Home* (HarperTrophy, 1982) GRL: J; RL: 2.5
- *Small Pig* (HarperTrophy, 1986) GRL: I; RL: 1.8
- *Uncle Elephant* (HarperTrophy, 1986) GRL: J; RL: 2.5

Each of these books has approximately 80 pages and most have five chapters. (One book has four chapters; one book has six chapters.) If you choose one of those two books, you will have to decide what to do about an extra day for the extra chapter. (You can reread a favorite chapter if a group is one chapter short or omit one chapter if a group has one more than the others.)

Whole–Class Book for Day 1 (or Days 1-5, depending on your format):
- *Frog and Toad Are Friends* (HarperTrophy, 1979) GRL: K; RL: 2.4

Frog and Toad Are Friends has five short chapters about Frog and Toad and their special friendship. Each chapter can be treated as a separate story to be read each day during a school week. The text is well suited for children who are ready to begin reading easy chapter books. (There are some second-grade basal textbooks that include a chapter from *Frog and Toad Are Friends*. If this is your situation, then use the story in your basal textbook for Day 1, then go to Day 2 if you have *Frog and Toad Are Friends* books for all of your students, or skip to the Book Club Groups.)

[Arnold Lobel]

Purpose

For students to identify story elements from the text and complete a Story Map after reading the text

Before:	Give a little talk about Frog and Toad and have children look at the pictures in the book.
During:	The children will echo read the first story about Frog and Toad to tell you what happens in this story.
After:	Discuss these two friends and what happened in this story.

Preparation/Materials Needed

- *Frog and Toad Are Friends* by Arnold Lobel—one copy per student (Or, partner read if you have enough copies for half of the class.)
- A Story Map (page 185) written on chart paper with colorful markers

Before Reading

Before students are asked to read the book on the first day, discuss how a story, or fiction, is usually organized in a particular way. Discuss how knowing this information can help a reader understand a story better and a Story Map offers a method of organizing the information in each story. Tell students, "Today, we are going to look at how stories are organized. Most stories have the same basic format—you learn about the characters, the setting, and what happens at the beginning, middle, and end. We will use a Story Map to identify the story elements in the first chapter of Arnold Lobel's book *Frog and Toad Are Friends*. We will work together to fill in the Story Map after we read this chapter."

Display the cover of *Frog and Toad Are Friends*. Ask students to predict what they think the story might be about. Show students the chart paper Story Map. Fill in the Title and Author sections of the Story Map together.

Take a picture walk through the first chapter and talk about the two characters you see in this chapter. ("Which do you think is Frog? Which one do you think is Toad?") Then, talk about the setting—where the story takes place. Ask students, "Do any of you know what you call the time and place that a story occurs?" If needed, discuss the settings of stories you have read previously. Have students identify the settings of several of these stories. If possible, have the books available to show the class so that students can see how the pictures help identify the setting.

Tell students, "Today, when you are echo reading, pay attention to the setting of this story so that we can write it down on the Story Map. Also, pay attention to the beginning, middle, and end. We will discuss and write these elements when we finish the first chapter of this book."

During Reading

If you are teaching first grade, read *Frog and Toad Are Friends* in a whole-class, echo reading format, stopping as soon as the setting is evident. Have students help you list the characters and setting (when and where the story happened) on the chart. Tell students, "We will now finish reading the first chapter, Spring, to fill in the rest of the Story Map. We need to remember what happens at the beginning, middle, and end of this chapter or story." As you finish reading the first chapter, stop three times to summarize what

[Arnold Lobel]

has happened at the beginning, middle, and end of this story, or chapter, with students.

If you are teaching second or third grade, have each student take turns reading aloud a page from the chapter with a partner. When the partners have finished reading this chapter, should talk about the characters, setting, and what happened at the beginning, middle, and end of the story. When most of the partners have finished reading and discussing the story, have students help you list the characters and setting (when and where the story happened) on the chart paper Story Map. Tell students, "You will now finish reading the first chapter, Spring, then we will fill in the rest of the Story Map. You will need to know what happens at the beginning, middle, and end of this chapter or story."

Purpose

For students to identify story elements from the text and complete a Story Map after reading the second chapter of the text (and continue doing this for each of the four remaining chapters)

Before:	Review the Story Map and read to fill it in after reading the second (third, fourth, or fifth) chapter.
During:	Read a page each with your group (or echo read if that would be better).
After:	Fill in the Story Map for each story or chapter or toss the beach ball.

After Reading

Review what happened in the story. Start by saying, "Let's see if we can think of a sentence to summarize the beginning of this chapter." Continue in the same way with the middle and end of the story. If time permits, discuss the friendship of Frog and Toad from the story. Discuss how both Frog and Toad show friendship to each other.

The whole class can read the class book one chapter per day (Days 2–5) or each of four randomly assigned groups can read a chapter and finish the class book on the second day.

Preparation/Materials Needed

- *Frog and Toad Are Friends* by Arnold Lobel—one copy per student or enough copies to partner read if you will complete the next four chapters as a class
- A chart of partners if partner reading the next four chapters (students will stay with their partners for four days unless there is a problem.) A chart of groups for today's work (teacher assigned) with the leader's name if reading all four chapters today.
- Story Maps written on chart paper or transparencies and colored markers or pens

[Arnold Lobel]

Before Reading

Review the chapter, "Spring," read on Day 1. Review the Story Map with students. Let each student know that he will be working on a new Story Map for each of the remaining chapters, which are separate stories. Tell students that each day after reading with their partners, they will talk about what they think belongs on the Story Map for that chapter.

If you have decided to finish the book in four groups with each group reading one of the remaining chapters, tell students that after reading their chapters with their groups, they should discuss what goes on the Story Map. Each group will come up with their own Story Map for each chapter. If they do this in groups, then each group will complete the same chart as the whole group completed yesterday. Pass out one chart-paper Story Map for each group and assign each group one of the remaining chapters: "The Story," "A Lost Button," "A Swim," or "The Letter." Fill out the first part of the chart together—title (*Frog and Toad Are Friends*) and author (Arnold Lobel).

During Reading—Small Groups

Divide students into four groups, assigning each group a leader and one of the remaining chapters. Group members will take turns reading aloud one page to the group. When the chapter is read, they will talk about the story elements on the Story Map. Monitors and coach the group as they read and discuss the story elements.

During Reading—Whole Class

Have students read one chapter per day for the next four days, using the same format from Day 1 (whole-class echo reading or partner reading). Remind them to fill out a new Story Map for each chapter.

After Reading

Give students in each group time to write and then share their Story Map charts. Let each group tell the whole class about their characters, setting, and the beginning, middle, and end of each chapter. If time permits, let students toss the beach ball.

[Arnold Lobel]

If you are reading one chapter per day as a class, this will be Day 6.

Purpose

For students to preview the four books selected for the Book Club Groups, then list first, second, and third choices for Book Club Groups

Before:	Talk about the four books selected and how to preview books and make choices for Book Club Groups.
During:	Have children read a page or two from each of the four books.
After:	Have children write selections on index cards or pieces of paper.

Preparation/Materials Needed

- A list of children randomly assigned to four groups
- Student copies (five to seven) of the four books to be previewed are placed in the four corners of the room, in baskets around the room, or at tables so that students can preview them—one title per corner, basket, or table.
- Index cards/pieces of paper and pencils/pens to write Book Club Group choices

Before Reading

Randomly assign children to one of four groups. Then, choose a leader for each of the four Book Club Groups. Tell students, "Today, you will have a chance to preview the four books you will get to choose from for our Book Club Groups. Arnold Lobel is the author of all four books.

You may like one or two of the books better than others. Your job today is to find a book you want to read—one that interests you. But remember, it must also be a book you can read—one in which you already know most of the words. (You may need to teach the "five finger rule"—more than five words missed on a page means the book will probably be too hard to read.)

During Reading

Tell students, "Today, you will move from table to table (corner to corner, basket to basket, etc.) to preview each of our Book Club Group selections. You will have five minutes to preview each book. First, look at the pictures to see what the book is about and whether it looks interesting. Next, see if you can read it. When the five minutes are up, I will give you a signal (set a timer for five minutes or use the classroom clock and ring a bell) and then you will move to the next table (corner, basket, etc.). Each group will visit all four tables (corners, baskets, etc.) looking at the books and reading a page or two of each book." Begin the process and after five minutes, have the groups rotate to the next set of books. Do this until all four groups have previewed all four books.

After Reading

Display the covers of the four books selected for the Book Club Groups. Then, have students select the three books they would like to read. Ask them to write their first, second, and third choices on index cards or pieces of paper. Collect the lists from students and use their lists to create the Book Club Groups.

[Arnold Lobel]

Purpose

For students to read and discuss the first chapter of their books with their groups

Before:	Talk about how students will read the first chapters of their books today. Review the Story Map and have students look for the story elements in their first stories or chapters.
During:	Have each child read a page from her book to the group. Let the leader help with echo reading, if needed.
After:	Have children talk about the story elements with their class.

Preparation/Materials Needed

- Create and post a list of the Book Club Groups; highlight the name of the leader of each group.
- Student copies (five to seven) of the four books

- Story Map (page 185) to refer to when discussing the story elements after the first chapter is read

Before Reading

Meet with the entire class to map out the next five days of reading with your Book Club Groups. Go over the procedures for Book Club Groups: How will they read? What does the leader do? What happens if a student does not know a word? What do they do when they finish? What will they do after they read the first chapter so that they can begin to discuss it with their groups?

During Reading

Students will work together to read the first chapter and then discuss the characters, setting, what happened in this chapter. Monitor and coach the groups, noting and praising students when they read well, and also when they identify story elements.

After Reading

Meet back as a whole class to discuss the story each group is reading. Have students take note of similarities and differences in the stories.

[Arnold Lobel]

Purpose

For students to complete group Story Maps after reading chapters in books by Arnold Lobel

Before:	Talk about how students will read the second chapters of their books today. Review the Story Map and have students look for the story elements in their second stories or chapters.
During:	Have each child read a page from his book to the group. Let the leader help with echo reading, if needed.
After:	Have children talk about the story elements with their groups.

Preparation/Materials Needed:

- Chart paper Story Map—one copy for each group
- Student copies (five to seven) of the four books

Before Reading

Discuss any problems groups may be having completing their charts. Have students discuss their strategies for reading and completing their charts today. Remind each group to write a short summary of the beginning, middle, and end of the chapter on the Story Map.

During Reading

Instruct children to read this chapter with their groups. Then, have students work together to complete the Story Maps. Monitor and coach the groups, noting and praising students as they identify story elements.

After Reading

Have the class meet as a whole group to discuss the story each of the four groups is reading with their Book Club Group. Have students share their charts.

[Arnold Lobel]

Purpose

For students to complete group Story Maps after reading chapters in books by Arnold Lobel

Before:	Talk about how students will read the third chapters of their books today. Review the Story Map and have students look for the story elements in their third stories or chapters.
During:	Have each child read a page from her book to the group. Let the leader help with echo reading, if needed.
After:	Have children write and talk about the story elements with their groups.

Preparation/Materials Needed

- Chart paper Story Maps—one copy for each group

- Student copies (five to seven) of the four books

Before Reading

Discuss any problems groups may be having completing their charts. Have students discuss their strategies for reading and completing their charts today. Remind each group to write a short summary of the beginning, middle, and end of their chapter on a chart paper Story Map.

During Reading

Tell children to read this chapter with their groups. Then, have each group work together to complete their Story Map. Monitor and coach the groups, noting and praising students as they identify story elements.

After Reading

Gather the class to meet as a whole group to discuss the story each of the four groups is reading with their Book Club Group. Have a student from each group share the chart paper Story Map.

[Arnold Lobel]

Purpose

For students to complete group Story Maps after reading chapters in books by Arnold Lobel

Before:	Talk about how students will read the fourth chapters of their books today. Review the Story Map and have students look for the story elements in their fourth stories or chapters.
During:	Have each child read a page from his book to the group. Let the leader help with echo reading, if needed.
After:	Have children talk about the story elements with their class.

Preparation/Materials Needed

- Chart paper Story Maps—one copy for each group

- Student copies (five to seven) of the four books

Before Reading

Discuss any problems groups may be having completing their charts. Have students discuss their strategies for reading and completing their charts today. Remind each group to write a short summary of the beginning, middle, and end of the chapter on the chart paper Story Map.

During Reading

Have children read this chapter with their groups, and then work together to complete the Story Maps. Monitor and coach the groups, noting and praising students as they identify story elements.

After Reading

Get the class back together as a whole group to discuss the story each of the four groups is reading. Have a student from each group share the chart paper Story Map.

[Arnold Lobel]

Purpose

For students to complete Story Maps after reading chapters in books by Arnold Lobel

Before:	Talk about how students will read the fifth chapters of their books today. Review the Story Map and have students look for the story elements in their fifth stories or chapters.
During:	Have each child read a page from her book to the group. Let the leader help with echo reading, if needed.
After:	Have children talk about the story elements with the class.

Preparation/Materials Needed

• Chart paper Story Maps—one copy for each group

• Student copies (five to seven) of the four books

Before Reading

Discuss any problems the groups may be having completing their charts. Have students discuss their strategies for reading and completing the group charts today. Remind each group to write a short summary of the beginning, middle, and end of the chapter on the chart paper Story Map.

During Reading

Instruct children to read the final chapter with their groups. Then, have students work together in their groups to complete the chart paper Story Maps. Monitor and coach the groups, noting and praising students as they identify story elements.

After Reading

Have the class meet as a whole group to discuss the story each of the four groups is reading. Have a student from each group share the chart paper Story Map.

[Arnold Lobel]

Extensions

Self-Selected Reading

- Make a variety of Arnold Lobel's books available for students to read during Self-Selected Reading time.

Guided Reading

- Make the chart paper Story Maps available to students as they read other texts.

Writing

- Encourage students to write about friends they have.
- Model for students how a Story Map can help them write a summary of a book.
- Now that students are reading chapter books, talk about and model writing a chapter book (maybe about two friends).

Working with Words

- Do a Making Words lesson with the word, **friends**.

  Letters: e, i, d, f, n, r, s
  Make: if is rid red end ends/send/dens Fred fires/fries friends
  Sort: beginning sounds—s, d, fr; spelling patterns—-ed, -end; plurals
  Transfer: bled, sped, spend, blend

[chapter 2]

Author: Laura Numeroff

Laura Numeroff was born in Brooklyn, New York. She is the author of more than a dozen books for children. *If You Give a Mouse a Cookie* and *If You Give a Moose a Muffin*, illustrated by Felicia Bond, appear in some of the basal textbooks and anthologies for the end of first grade or second grade. In addition to the *If You Give a . . .* series, her books include *The Chicken Sisters* (HarperTrophy, 1999), *Mouse Cookies* (Laura Geringer, 1995), *Dogs Don't Wear Sneakers* (Aladdin Paperbacks, 1996), and *Laura Numeroff's 10-Step Guide to Living with Your Monster* (Laura Geringer, 2002). Laura Numeroff now lives in Brentwood, California.

Suggested Laura Numeroff books for the Book Club Groups:
- *If You Give a Moose a Muffin* (HarperCollins, 1991) GRL: K; RL: 2.7
- *If You Give a Mouse a Cookie* (HarperCollins, 1985) GRL: K; RL: 1.8
- *If You Give a Pig a Pancake* (HarperCollins, 1998) GRL: G; RL: 2.8
- *If You Take a Mouse to School* (HarperCollins, 2002) GRL: K; RL: 2.3

There is not a great deal of difference in the reading levels of the four books. Children can use the pictures in each book to help with words they cannot decode in isolation. So, show your young readers how to use context, picture clues, and beginning letter sounds to figure out unknown words.

[56]

[Laura Numeroff]

Purpose

For students to look at the four possible Book Club Group books and decide which book each student would like to read and can read

Before:	Model how to select a book.
During:	Have students preview books, reading a page or two from each of the four books.
After:	Have students list book choices and discuss the books they liked with their groups, then with the class.

Preparation/Materials Needed

- A list of children randomly assigned to four groups
- Student copies (five to seven) of the four books to be previewed are placed in the four corners of the room, in baskets around the room, or at tables so that students can preview them—one title per corner, basket, or table.
- Index cards/pieces of paper and pencils/pens to write Book Club Group choices

Before Reading

Randomly assign children to four groups. Choose a leader for each of the four groups. Tell students, "Today, you will have a chance to preview the four books you will get to choose from for our Book Club Groups. Laura Numeroff is the author of all four books. You may like one or two of the books better than others. Your job today is to find a book you want to read—one that interests you. But, remember it must also be a book you can read—one in which you already know most of the words. (You may need to teach the "five-finger rule"—more than five words missed on a page means the book will probably be too hard to read.)

During Reading

Do a short picture walk through each book, talking about the main character (either mouse, moose, or pig) and what is happening in the book. Tell students, "Today, you will move from table to table (corner to corner, basket to basket, etc.) to preview each of the four Book Club Group selections. You will have five minutes to preview each book. First, look at the pictures in the book to see what the book is about and whether it looks interesting. Next, see if you can read it. When the five minutes are up, I will give you a signal (set a timer for five minutes or use the classroom clock and ring a bell) and then you will move to the next table (corner, basket, etc.).

After Reading

Let students discuss the books they liked with their groups, then the class. Give each student an index card or piece of paper to list his first, second, and third choices. Then, have students give you the index cards so that you can make Book Club Group assignments.

[Laura Numeroff]

Purpose

For students to read their books and make a list of the consequences for each action

Before:	Talk about the characters in each book and the consequences of the actions.
During:	Have students read the books in an echo reading format (or partners) and discuss them.
After:	Let groups share their lists of what happened.

Preparation/Materials Needed

- Student copies (five to seven) of each book for Book Club Groups
- Create and post the Book Club Groups from the choices the students wrote on their index cards or papers.
- Chart paper and a magic marker for each group to make a list of the consequences they come across in their book

Before Reading

Tell students, "Today, you will meet in your Book Club Groups for the first time." Talk about the Book Club Groups and how each group will read a different book and find out the consequences of giving a mouse a cookie, giving a moose a muffin, giving a pig a pancake, or taking a mouse to school. The picture walk and the book previews gave students some idea of what happened. Now, have each group read their book and make a list of consequences for each action to share with the class. Tell children, "Find out the consequences of giving a mouse a cookie, giving a moose a muffin, giving a pig a pancake, or taking a mouse to school. After each page, the leader will ask the group what happened and what needs to be added to the list, so think about this as you listen to each page."

During Reading

Have students work together in their groups to read the selected books (echo reading, partner reading, or reading by themselves, depending on the grade level and reading levels of students in your class). If students are reading out loud, each student in the group should read two pages out loud starting with the leader and going around the group clockwise. After every student reads two pages tell the leader to ask what, if anything, to add to the list. If there is something to add to the list he should add it. As students are reading, walk around the room, "dropping an ear" and listening, monitoring and coaching the groups as they read and add consequences to their charts.

After Reading

Bring the class back to a large group setting and have a member of each group (it can be the leader or another good reader) share with the class the list of consequences written on the group's chart paper.

[Laura Numeroff]

Purpose

For students to reread their books and talk about the main character in each of the four books

Before:	Talk about the main character in each book and tell students to reread the books.
During:	Have children reread their books with their Book Club Groups, using the same during-reading strategy as yesterday (can be read out loud, partner reading, or echo reading).
After:	Have each group come up with a sentence or two about the main character in their book and share it with the class.

Preparation/Materials Needed

- Student copies (five to seven) of each book
- Large chart paper and dark-colored marker for each group to write a sentence about the character in their story

Before Reading

Tell students, "Today, after reading, each group will create a sentence or two that tells about the main character in your book." Remind children of a time you have done this with the whole class after reading a book or story or of a time you modeled this in your Writing mini-lesson. Make sure to stress that when they write a sentence or two they don't want to tell too much, just enough so that everyone will know about the character. They do not have to include everything the character does.

During Reading

Students will reread their books with their groups. (Rereading helps fluency.) Model for students how to read a page out loud, beginning with the leader, and how the leader begins the discussion of what happened in this book. Then, as a group, students will complete a character summary. Monitor and coach the Book Club Groups. Help those groups that need help writing a sentence or two about their book characters. (To avoid this problem, select a leader for each group who is a strong reader and writer.)

After Reading

Bring the students back to a whole-class setting and let each Book Club Group share the sentences about the main character.

[Laura Numeroff]

Extensions

Self-Selected Reading

- Read some of Laura Numeroff's other books during the teacher read-aloud.
- Encourage children to read books they did not read during Book Club Groups.

Writing

- Encourage students to write about what might happen to them if someone gave them cookies, muffins, or pancakes. Have them think about Numeroff's style of writing and how it can help them to write this piece.
- Do an interactive Writing mini-lesson and develop a story with the class. Then, let students try it on their own.
- During your Writing mini-lesson, write a summary of one of Numeroff's books.
- Have students write about the main characters in Numeroff's books and tell what they liked or didn't like about these characters.

Art

- Have students draw pictures of the main characters or their favorite parts in the books.
- Have students make sock puppets (like the moose did in *If You Give a Moose a Muffin*).

Guided Reading

- Let children choose whether to draw pictures of their characters or write about the characters after reading.

Working with Words

- Make up four sentences, one from each book, and use them for a Guess the Covered Word activity. For example:

  1. After you give a mouse a cookie, he may want some **milk**.
  2. If you give a moose a muffin, he may want some **blackberries**.
  3. If you give a pig a pancake, she may want some **stamps**.
  4. If you take a mouse to school, he may ask for a **lunch box**.

- Do a Making Words lesson with the word, **muffins**.

  Letters: i, u, f, f, m, n, s
  Make: is in fin fun sun sum fins muff muffs snuff sniff minus muffins
  Sort: beginning sounds—f, s, sn; spelling patterns—-un, -uff; plurals
  Transfer: win, stuff, shin, cuff

- Do a Making Words lesson with the word, **pancakes**.

  Letters: a, a, e, c, k, n, p, s
  Make: as an nap/pan span/snap neck peck pack sack peak speak sneak/snake snack speck pancakes
  Sort: beginning sounds—p, sn, sp; spelling patterns—-ap, -ack, -eak, -an, -eck
  Transfer: trap, track, deck, leak

[Laura Numeroff]

• Do a Rounding up the Rhymes lesson with Laura Numeroff's book *Chimps Don't Wear Glasses* (Scholastic, Inc., 1995).

1. Read the book to the class during a teacher read-aloud and enjoy the funny rhymes.

2. During a second reading, read the first three pages of text and "round up" or find the words that rhyme: **cook**, **book**. Write these words on index cards and put them in a pocket chart, or write them on a transparency, chalkboard, or white board.

3. Read the next two pages of text and find/write the rhymes: **cars**, **jars**.

4. Read the next two pages of text and find/write the rhymes: **shop**, **mop**.

5. Read the next three pages of text and find/write the rhymes: **kites**, **sights**.

6. Read the next three pages of text and find/write the rhymes: **mugs**, **pugs**.

7. Read the next two pages of text and find/write the rhymes: **mind**, **find**.

8. Read the next two pages of text and find/write the rhymes: **floats**, **boats**.

9. Read the final three pages and find/write the two sets of rhymes: **stilts**, **quilts** and **dine**, **mine**.

10. Get rid of the pair of rhymes that does not have the same rime (spelling pattern): **kites**, **sights**.

11. Use the remaining patterns to do some transfer words.

Ask students, "What if you came to this word when reading (h**ook**)? What pattern would help you figure it out (**cook**/b**ook**)?"

Do more reading transfers with two or three of these words: st**ars** (**cars**/j**ars**); dr**op** (m**op**/sh**op**); pl**ugs** (m**ugs**/p**ugs**); k**ind** (m**ind**/f**ind**); g**oats** (fl**oats**/b**oats**); k**ilts** (st**ilts**/q**uilts**); sp**ine** (d**ine**/m**ine**).

Ask students, "What if you wanted to write this word (sh**ook**)? What pattern would help you figure it out (**cook**/b**ook**)?"

Do more writing transfers with two or three of these words: b**ars** (**cars**/j**ars**); cr**op** (m**op**/sh**op**); r**ugs** (m**ugs**/p**ugs**); w**ind** (m**ind**/f**ind**); c**oats** (fl**oats**/b**oats**); w**ilts** (st**ilts**/q**uilts**); f**ine** (d**ine**/m**ine**).

Author: Peggy Parrish

Peggy Parrish (1927-1988) was originally from Manning, South Carolina and taught school in Texas, Oklahoma, Kentucky, and New York. She wrote many books for children of all ages, and among the favorites of teachers and children are her books about a literal-minded housekeeper named Amelia Bedelia. Amelia Bedelia was created in 1963, and Peggy Parrish wrote a total of 12 books about the zany antics of this beloved housekeeper. These "I can read books" are wonderful to use in the primary grades, especially second grade, when talking about the multiple meanings of some words. Each time Amelia is told to do something, she tries her best and does exactly what she is told to do, but things never turn out quite right. Amelia does, however, make readers laugh as she gets things mixed up, and she does end up making other characters happy. Young children enjoy finding out what Amelia does and how she gets out of trouble.

Suggested Peggy Parrish/*Amelia Bedelia* Books for Book Club Groups (choose four):
- *Amelia Bedelia* (HarperTrophy, 1992) GRL: L; RL: 2.5
- *Amelia Bedelia and the Baby* (Avon, 1996) GRL: L; RL: 2.1
- *Amelia Bedelia and the Surprise Shower* (HarperTrophy, 1995) GRL: L; RL: 2.2
- *Amelia Bedelia Goes Camping* (HarperTrophy, 2003) GRL: L; RL: 1.5
- *Amelia Bedelia Helps Out* (Avon, 1997) GRL: L; RL: 1.8
- *Amelia Bedelia's Family Album* (HarperTrophy, 2003) GRL: L; RL: 2.5
- *Come Back, Amelia Bedelia* (HarperTrophy, 1995) GRL: L; RL: 2.7
- *Good Work, Amelia Bedelia* (HarperTrophy, 2003) GRL: L; RL: 2.5
- *Play Ball, Amelia Bedelia* (HarperTrophy, 1996) GRL: L; RL: 2.8
- *Teach Us, Amelia Bedelia* (Scholastic, Inc., 2003) GRL: L; RL: 2.8
- *Thank You, Amelia Bedelia* (HarperTrophy, 1993) GRL: L; RL: 2.8

[Peggy Parrish]

According to the publisher (HarperTrophy), the readability of these *Amelia Bedelia* books is second grade as determined by the Frye readability formula. Some of the books are longer than others, and these longer books might be thought of as "harder books." Since children have the same amount of time to read all of the books, the more fluent readers can read the extra pages in the same amount of time. One easier book is probably *Amelia Bedelia's Family Album* because it has 10-20 pages less to read than the other selections. If you put your second or third graders in heterogeneous groups, they will be able to read and enjoy any and all of these! The focus of the Book Club Groups will be the multiple meanings of words—what is meant and what Amelia does.

Purpose

To give a short book talk about the four selected *Amelia Bedelia* books and to model for children how to decide what books they would like to read when they preview the four Book Club Group texts

Before:	Give a book talk about each of the selections and model how to preview the books.
During:	Let students take picture walks through all four books and read a few pages.
After:	Have children make selections for Book Club Groups.

Preparation/Materials Needed

- A list of children randomly assigned to four groups

- Student copies (five to seven) of the four books to be previewed are placed in the four corners of the room, in baskets around the room, or at tables so that students can preview them—one title per corner, basket, or table.
- Index cards/pieces of paper and pencils/pens to write Book Club Group choices

Before Reading

Tell students, "Today, you will have a chance to preview the books, and then you will get to choose which of the four books you would like to read with a Book Club Group. Amelia Bedelia is the main character in all of these books written by Peggy Parrish. I will do a short picture walk through each of the four books, talking about Amelia Bedelia and what is happening." (Do this now using each of the four books you have chosen for your class to read.)

"Now, you will have a chance to preview all four of the books and get to choose your first, second, and third choices for your Book Club Groups. You may like one or two of the books better than the others, or you may like them all!

"Your job today is to find a book you want to read—one that interests you. But, remember it must also be a book you can read—one in which you know most of the words. (If you have taught the "five-finger rule" then remind them of it. See page 19 for more on the "five-finger rule".) So, as you look through each book today, be thinking, 'Is this a book about Amelia Bedelia that I would like to read? Can I read this book all by myself?'"

[Peggy Parrish]

During Reading

Assign students randomly to four groups; choose a leader for each group. Tell students, "Today, you will move from table to table (corner to corner, basket to basket, etc.) to preview each of our Book Club Group selections. You will have five minutes to preview each book. First, look at the pictures to see what the book is about and if it looks interesting. Next, see if you can read it. When five minutes are up, I will give you a signal (set a timer for five minutes, or use the classroom clock and ring a bell or blink the lights) and then you will move to the next table (corner, basket, etc.). Each group will visit all four tables (corners, baskets, etc.) reading a page or two of each book." Begin the process and after five minutes, have the groups rotate to the next set of books. Do this until all four groups have previewed all four books.

After Reading

Display the covers of the books selected for the Book Club Groups. Have students spend a minute or two thinking about the books and which ones they like the best. Then, have each student select the three books he would like to read by writing his first, second, and third choices on an index card. Collect the students' lists and use them to create the Book Club Groups.

[Peggy Parrish]

Purpose

For students to begin to read *Amelia Bedelia* books and talk about multiple-meaning words

Before:	Assign Book Club Groups with leaders noted. Tell students what they will read, how they will read, and what they will do after reading. Discuss multi-meaning words.
During:	Have each child read a page to his group, stopping halfway through the books.
After:	Let students discuss characters, setting, and what the story is about in each *Amelia Bedelia* book. Have each group find at least two multi-meaning words.

Preparation/Materials Needed

- A chart that lists students randomly assigned to four groups
- Student copies (five to seven) of the four books to be previewed are placed in the four corners of the room, in baskets around the room, or at tables so that students can preview them—one title per corner, basket, or table. Place a paper clip at a good stopping place in each book, approximately halfway through the book.
- A chart to help groups remember what to discuss after reading (See During Reading.)

Before Reading

Show students the chart of the four Book Club Groups and their assignments. Use asterisks or other indicators to show which students are leaders. Discuss how words can have more than one meaning. Give the children some examples they are familiar with, such as dear/deer, two/to/too, and mail/male. Tell children that, as they read their books today, they need to be aware of the characters, the setting, and what is happening in the books. Remind them that when reading *Amelia Bedelia* books they need to pay attention to the words that Amelia mixes up and the different meanings of these words. These are the things they will discuss in their groups after reading and then tell to the whole class.

During Reading

Ask students to take turns reading a page each to their groups until they get to the paper clips. Instruct the group leaders to begin the read-aloud process and act as the "teacher" by helping any students who need help. When each group is finished reading, have them discuss all of the characters in their book besides Amelia Bedelia, the setting, and what is happening. Finally, have students find two examples of words with more than one meaning and talk about what was really meant and what Amelia did. Be sure that someone in the group completes the chart, filling in the information on the title, characters, setting, problem, and multiple-meaning words. (See the example below.)

Amelia Bedelia Book: _____

Characters: _____

Setting: _____

Problem: _____

Multi-Meaning Words: _____ , _____

After Reading

Let one member of each group share her group's findings about characters, setting, problem, and words. The group presenter may use the completed chart as a reminder.

[Peggy Parrish]

Purpose

For students to find out how Amelia Bedelia gets out of trouble and to learn or review how to retell a story using pictures

Before:	Model how to retell the story using the pictures in the book.
During:	Have each child read a page to her group, finishing the book.
After:	Let students discuss what happened at the beginning, middle, and end of each *Amelia Bedelia* book.

Preparation/Materials Needed

* Student copies (five to seven) of the chosen books with a paper clip at a good stopping place in each book, approximately halfway through the book.

Before Reading

Remind students that they will finish the books they are reading with their Book Club Groups to find out whether Amelia gets in trouble and, if she does, how she gets out of it. Use an *Amelia Bedelia* book they are not reading to show children how they can use the pictures as retelling prompts. Then, model this strategy by using a few pages in the book to show the problem and a few sentences (your own words, not from the book!) to explain the problem and how Amelia solves it.

During Reading

In their assigned Book Club Groups, have students finish their books, taking turns reading aloud one page at a time. Go from group to group, "dropping an ear" and listening and helping as needed. When each group is finished, the group should begin discussing how Amelia solved her problem. Monitor the groups to make sure each one is using pictures and telling about the solution—not reading it. Be sure the groups mention how Amelia solved her problem.

After Reading

Ask each group to select one student who will share what happens in the group's book by using the pictures in the book to retell the beginning, middle, and end. Be sure that each group presenter mentions how Amelia solved her problem.

[Peggy Parrish]

Purpose

For students to compare the books and find and reread their favorite parts of the books

Before:	Review the books and compare characters, settings, and problems.
During:	Have students reread their favorite parts silently. (Rereading helps fluency!)
After:	Have children draw their favorite parts.

Preparation/Materials Needed

- Student copies (five to seven) of the chosen books
- Chart from Day 2
- Drawing paper, colorful markers, crayons, and/or colored pencils

Before Reading

Lead a discussion of the stories using the chart from Day 2. (See page 65.) Add two new lines.

Amelia Bedelia Book _____

Characters: _____

Setting: _____

Problem: _____

Multi-Meaning Words : _____, _____

Solution: _____

Favorite Part: _____

Explain that today, students will find and reread their favorite parts of the books. After reading, they will draw pictures of their favorite parts and share them with the whole class.

During Reading

Ask children to find and silently reread their favorite parts. They can read their favorite parts to other group members when everyone in the group is finished reading and they are waiting for the other groups to finish.

After Reading

Ask children to draw pictures of their favorite parts of the books. Each child will illustrate her favorite part. One idea is to have each student write the following at the bottom of the page before illustrating: My favorite part was when _____. When children are finished drawing, they can share their illustrations with the whole class, or you can bind their illustrations together and make a class book.

[Peggy Parrish]

Self-Selected Reading

- Read some of Peggy Parrish's other books for your teacher read-aloud.
- Encourage children to read books during Self-Selected Reading that they did not read during Book Club Groups.

Writing

- Encourage students to write stories with multiple–meaning words.
- For an interactive Writing mini-lesson, develop an *Amelia Bedelia* story with your class, and then let them try it on their own.
- During a Writing mini-lesson, write a summary of one of the *Amelia Bedelia* books.

Guided Reading

- Let children choose whether to draw or write about their favorite characters or books after reading.
- Have children "Do the Book." Assign children to be the characters (Amelia, Mr. and Mrs., etc.) and put on a play. This is not an elaborate play. Use hats or name necklaces for the characters, and Amelia simply needs an apron.

Working with Words

- Do a Making Words lesson with the name, **Amelia**.

  Letters: a, a, e, i, l, m
  Make: me Ma/am aim ail elm lame/male lime/mile mail meal Amelia
  Sort: beginning sounds—l, m; multiple-meaning words—male/mail; spelling pattern—-ail
  Transfer: pail, jail, trail, snail

- Do a Making Words lesson with the word, **surprise**.

  Letters: e, i, u, p, r, r, s, s
  Make: is us use/Sue sip rip ripe rise sure pure rises super/purse purses surprise
  Sort: beginning sounds—r, s; spelling patterns—-ip, -ure
  Transfer: clip, snip, slip

Author: Patricia Polacco

Patricia Polacco is another popular author of children's books. She is the author of the award winning *The Keeping Quilt* (Aladdin Paperbacks, 1988), *Just Plain Fancy* (Dragonfly Books, 1990), and other favorites. She grew up in a family of artists and storytellers and writes about the many cultures she came in contact with while growing up. Patricia Polacco shares her family's life in Michigan, and the favorite people in her life through her writing. Some of her books demonstrate personal triumphs and disappointments of her family members, as well as the love that reached across the ocean, land, and generations. Ms. Polacco writes a variety of stories for elementary children. Many have humor in them, and some are serious; all teach respect for family and friends. Patricia Polacco's artwork often interprets the story with style and panache. Her lively characters are bright and expressive and become real to her young readers. Her stories seem just right for third graders. Ms. Polacco spends a great deal of time visiting schools and talking to children about her books. She and her family now live in Oakland, California.

Suggested Patricia Polacco Books for Book Club Groups (choose four):
- *Appelemando's Dreams* (The Putnam & Grosset Group, 1997) GRL: M; RL: 5.4
- *Babushka's Doll* (Aladdin Books, 1990) GRL: P; RL: 3.3
- *Chicken Sunday* (The Putnam & Grosset Group, 1992) GRL: N; RL: 4.8
- *Just Plain Fancy* (Dragonfly Books, 1990) GRL: O; RL: 3.8
- *The Keeping Quilt* (Aladdin Paperbacks, 1988) GRL: M; RL: 5.3
- *My Rotten Redheaded Older Brother* (Aladdin Paperbacks, 1994) GRL: M; RL: 3.9
- *Mrs. Katz and Tush* (Dell Dragonfly Books, 1992) GRL: P; RL: 4.4
- *Picnic at Mudsock Meadow* (Trumpet, 1992) GRL: O; RL: 5.2
- *Rechenka's Eggs* (Penguin Putnam Books for Young Readers, 1996) GRL: M; RL: 3.5
- *Thunder Cake* (The Putnam & Grosset Group, 1997) GRL: M; RL: 3.5

[Patricia Polacco]

Purpose

For students to make predictions about the four books and decide what books they would like to read while previewing the four selections

Before:	Preview the (four) books with the class.
During:	Have each child look at and read a page or two from each of the four books.
After:	Have children select the books they want to read and write those choices on index cards.

Preparation/Materials Needed

- A list of children randomly assigned to four groups
- Student copies (five to seven) of the four books to be previewed are placed in the four corners of the room, in baskets around the room, or at tables so that students can preview them—one title per corner, basket, or table.
- Index cards/pieces of paper and pencils/pens to write Book Club Group choices

Before Reading

On the first day, begin the Guided Reading time by telling children that you have selected four Patricia Polacco books for them to read in Book Club Groups. If this is the first session using this format, you might talk about how grown-ups often read the same book and get together with friends to talk about the book. You might use Oprah's or some other book club as an example. Then, explain that they are such good readers that they are now ready for Book Club Groups with their classmates!

One at a time, show the cover of each book and using only the cover, get children thinking about what they know about these books and what they might read. Then, tell children that they only have three days to spend on these books and they don't have enough time or copies of the books for each child to read all four books. Each Book Club Group will read one book and hear about the other three books.

During Reading

Next, hand each child an index card and ask him to write his name and the numbers 1, 2, and 3 on the card. Explain that you will give them 20 minutes to preview the books—5 minutes for each book. Place all of the copies of each book in the four corners of the room (or on four tables, in four baskets, etc.). Randomly assign children to groups. Send group one to the first set of books, group two to the second set of books, etc. Set a timer for five minutes and tell the children that when the bell (buzzer, etc.) sounds, they must move to the next corner (table, basket, etc.) and the next group of books.

After Reading

When the 20 minutes are up, have children return to their seats and write their first, second, and third choices on the index cards. When they have trouble deciding which are their first choices and which are their second choices, tell them not to worry too much about the order of choices because you can't guarantee they will get their first choices or even their second choices. "I want the groups to be about the same size, and I need to put groups together that will work well together. I promise I will give you one of your choices and I will try to give you your first choice."

[Patricia Polacco]

Purpose
To introduce new vocabulary words to the class with Rivet and begin reading books

Before:	Introduce new vocabulary in these books with Rivet.
During:	Have children read the books and find how the new words are used in their stories.
After:	Have each group tell about what happened in their book and use the new words from the story in a meaningful sentence.

Preparation/Materials Needed
- Write blanks on the chalkboard, white board, or a transparency for each word. Choose two to three words from each book. (See Rivet instructions in Before Reading.)
- Create and post a list of the groups based on students' choices.
- Student copies (five to seven) of the chosen books
- Self-stick notes for students to mark places where they find these words

Before Reading
Use Rivet to introduce the vocabulary. Rivet is an activity created by Pat Cunningham (Cunningham and Hall, 1998, 2003; Cunningham, Hall, and Cunningham, 2000). Activating children's prior knowledge and getting them to make predictions before they read is one sure way to increase their involvement and comprehension. Rivet is an activity designed to accomplish this critical goal.

1. To prepare for a Rivet text introduction, choose 6–10 words from the text to be read. For Book Club Groups choose 2–3 words from each of your 4 chosen books. For the examples below, you may have to delete some words and add some other words, especially some of the important names in the books you choose.

For these examples, we have listed the words from the books (in bold), the definitions (in parentheses), and the number of blanks to draw on the board or transparency.

Bubbie (nickname for grandmother) 6
Babushka (Russian for grandmother or the scarf used around a woman's head) 8
handkerchief (piece of cloth used to blow your nose; old word, not always familiar to students) 12
quilt (a covering for the bed made from pieces of fabric sewn together) 5
Russian (a person who comes from or whose descendants came from Russia) 7
Passover (Jewish holiday near Easter) 8
spaseeba (Russian for "thank you") 8
chutzpah (you are not afraid) 8
sputtered (spit it out) 9
apologize (to say you are sorry or beg pardon) 9
unharnessed (to take off a horses gear) 11
community (people living together) 9
instructed (taught someone how to do something) 10
celebrated (observed with a ceremony) 10
canopy (overhead covering) 6
seder (Jewish religious meal) 5

[Patricia Polacco]

At the beginning of this Rivet activity, your board (or transparency) would look like this for the first eight words:

1. _ _ _ _ _ _
2. _ _ _ _ _ _ _ _
3. _ _ _ _ _ _ _ _ _ _ _ _
4. _ _ _ _ _
5. _ _ _ _ _ _ _
6. _ _ _ _ _ _ _
7. _ _ _ _ _ _ _
8. _ _ _ _ _ _ _

2. Fill in the letters to the first word one at a time, as the students watch.

1. B _ _ _ _ _

1. B u _ _ _ _

1. B u b _ _ _

1. B u b b _ _

1. B u b b i _

1. B u b b i e

Stop after each letter and see if anyone can guess the word. Students are not guessing letters but are trying to guess each word as soon as they think they know what it is. Most students could not guess the word when the board looks like this. But as the letters appear the words may become easier to figure out.

Continue with the remaining words.

3. Next, ask children to use these vocabulary words to predict something that might happen in these books.

(For example, "One book is about a **Russian** grandmother who celebrated **Passover**," or "One book is about something **celebrated** in the community under a **canopy**.")

Give students self-stick notes so that they can mark the place where they find these new words when they are reading. Model for children how you use a self-stick note when reading to mark a places you want to remember. Then, show them how they can use self-stick notes to find the place easily when returning to talk about the words with their group and then the whole class.

During Reading

Ask children to take turns reading aloud one page each with their Book Club Groups. Then, come up with two to three sentences so that students can see how the vocabulary words from their books are used in the stories. (Many classes may need to divide these stories in half by marking good stopping points with paper clips and then having students read to the paper clips. If this would be better for your class—Can they read the book in 20 minutes or do they need more time?—then do so.) As the groups read, walk around the room, "drop an ear" and listen to the groups. Are children reading fluently? Who is? Who isn't and needs extra coaching? Take notes if needed. These notes will help you when coaching one-on-one during Self-Selected Reading time. If one group is having more trouble than another, you may want to sit and work with that group for a while or plan on working with them during the Book Club Group reading tomorrow.

Are students using their self-stick notes to mark the new words? Have they found all of the vocabulary words in their books (or the first halves of their books)? Praise the groups that have and help the groups that need help. While children read, monitor and help, as needed.

[Patricia Polacco]

After Reading

Let children discuss the stories and vocabulary words they found in their books with their Book Club Groups. Then, with the whole class, let one member from each Book Club Group share the vocabulary words from the group's book in sentences, starting with the first word on the list. Make note of words the groups have not found. These words need to be talked about the next day. Remind students before reading to look for these words and after reading to talk about each word and give a sentence using it correctly.

Purpose

For students to talk about the expressions Patricia Polacco uses in her writing

Before:	Talk about expressions and some expressions your students know; finish words.
During:	Have children reread (or finish) their books and find expressions Polacco used to convey the language of the time or people.
After:	Finish the vocabulary words and have students use them in sentences. Then, have students talk about expressions in each of the four books.

Preparation/Materials Needed

- Student copies (five to seven) of the chosen books
- List of words not yet used in the books
- Self-stick notes
- Chart paper or a transparency on which to write the expressions used in the books

Before Reading

Talk about expressions, explaining what expressions are and why we use expressions in our speech and in books. Ask children to reread their books (or finish reading their books) with their groups to find these significant words or phrases to share with the class. Also, have children be on the lookout for any new words they have not shared with the class as they reread (or read the rest of) their books. They will need more self-stick notes to mark the pages with expressions or new words they have not shared. Have self-stick notes handy again and remind students how they used the notes yesterday.

[Patricia Polacco]

During Reading

Have groups reread or finish the books with partners and find any expressions in their stories. Monitor the groups or work with a group that needs extra help once you see that all groups are "on task." When the groups finish reading, have them discuss the expressions and words they found in their stories and select someone to share these with the whole class—it could be the leaders but it does not have to be.

After Reading

Have each group share an expression they found (maybe two) in their book and what the expression(s) means in everyday language. Some examples of expressions found in Patricia Polacco's books are:

Appelemando's Dreams

"He dreams the day away." (Appelemando daydreams all of the time.)

My Rotten Redheaded Brother

"Of course it is true, but it may not have happened." (The story could have happened but is not a true story.)

Babushka's Doll

"My stomach is making noises." (Natasha does not feel well. She has a stomachache.)

Mrs. Katz and Tush

". . . she has no tail—all you see is her tush." (The cat had no tail, so her rear end is visible.)

The Keeping Quilt

"The quilt welcomed me, Patricia, into the world . . . " (The quilt was put around Patricia, the author, when she was born.)

Chicken Sunday

"The next day we took a shortcut down the alley in back of the hat shop." (The three children took a shorter way to the hat shop, and it was down an alley in back of the hat shop.)

Chicken Sunday

"Chutzpah, you have chutzpah!" (You are not afraid; you are brave.)

Just Plain Fancy

"Please don't shun him," Naomi cried. (In this plain, Amish community, someone who is shunned is shamed in front of the older people—elders—then avoided by the community.)

Picnic at Mudsock Meadow

"Now William was really terribly and horribly mortified. And mad as the dickens." (William felt very bad and was very mad.)

[Patricia Polacco]

Extensions

Self-Selected Reading

- Read some of Patricia Polacco's other books for your teacher read-aloud.
- During Self-Selected Reading time, encourage children to read Patricia Polacco books they did not read during Book Club Groups.

Writing

- Encourage students to write stories about their families' histories using family expressions, if they know any.
- Do an interactive mini-lesson and develop a family story with the class. Then, let students try writing their own family stories.
- During a mini-lesson, write a book review (not a report but a review like those written for newspapers and magazines) of one of Patricia Polacco's books.

Art

- Let children choose to draw their favorite characters or parts from Patricia Polacco books after reading.

Guided Reading

- Let children use the three-possible-solutions strategy (and form) when reading other books or stories during Guided Reading. Have students work together in groups to read the selected books (echo reading, partner reading, or reading by themselves, depending on the grade level and reading levels of students in your class). While reading, group members identify the problems in their books.

Finally, each group discusses the problem and comes up with three possible solutions. Monitor and coach the groups or a group that may need extra help, noting and praising students as they identify problems and come up with three good solutions.

- Have children "do the book." Assign children to be characters or let the groups decide which children will be the characters in their books, and put on a series of plays. These are not elaborate plays. Use simple costumes or name necklaces for each character in the book.

Working with Words

- Do a Making Words lesson with the word, **grandmother**.

  Letters: a, e, o, d, g. h, m, n, r, r, t
  Make: an am arm/ram ran road rode roam groan grand anger moan armed other danger manger ranger another grandmother
  Sort: homophones—road/rode; spelling patterns—-am, -anger
  Transfer: clam, slam, stranger

- Do a Making Words lesson with the word, community.
  Letters: i, o, u, c, m, m, n, t, y
  Make: in it Mom Tom nut cut Tony tiny city unit unity mount count county commit community
  Sort: names—Mom, Tom, Tony; spelling patterns—-ut, -ount
  Transfer: shut, strut, amount

Author: Cynthia Rylant

Cynthia Rylant was raised in West Virginia where she found herself surrounded by hound dogs and barn cats. She has written some wonderful children's books about the area including *The Relatives Came* (Atheneum, 2001) and *When I Was Young in the Mountains* (E. P. Dutton, 1993). She also writes the popular, easy chapter books about a boy named Henry and his dog, Mudge. Rylant now lives in Oregon with her son, Nate, and two dogs and a cat. She says the idea for *Henry and Mudge* came from the time she owned a 200-pound English mastiff named Mudge. Her son, Nate, was seven at the time. Together, the two became *Henry and Mudge*. Cynthia Rylant has always loved dogs especially big, drooly, lovable dogs like Mudge.

Suggested Cynthia Rylant/*Henry and Mudge* Books for Book Club Groups (choose four):

- *Henry and Mudge and the Forever Sea* (Aladdin Paperbacks, 1993) GRL: J; RL: 2.2
- *Henry and Mudge and the Long Weekend* (Aladdin Paperbacks, 1996) GRL: J; RL: 2.5
- *Henry and Mudge and the Sneaky Crackers* (Aladdin Paperbacks, 1999) GRL: J; RL: 2.4
- *Henry and Mudge and the Snowman Plan* (Aladdin Paperbacks, 2000) GRL: J; RL: 2.1
- *Henry and Mudge in the Family Trees* (Aladdin Paperbacks, 1998) GRL: J; RL: 2.2
- *Henry and Mudge: The First Book* (Aladdin Paperback, 1990) GRL: J; RL: 2.2
- *Henry and Mudge under the Yellow Moon* (Aladdin Paperbacks, 1992) GRL: J; RL: 2.2

These easy chapter books have almost the same readability, but have different numbers of chapters and pages. Most of the books have 3 chapters and 40-48 pages, one has 4 chapters and 48 pages, and others have 5 and 7 chapters but only 40 pages. Most second graders can read these books independently or with partners if they need some help.

[Cynthia Rylant]

Purpose

For students to make predictions about the four books and decide which books to read while previewing the four possible Book Club Group selections

Before:	Preview the four books with the class.
During:	Have students preview the four selected books, reading a page or two from each.
After:	Let children select the books they want to read and write those choices on index cards.

Preparation/Materials Needed

- A list of children randomly assigned to four groups
- Student copies (five to seven) of the four books to be previewed are placed in the four corners of the room, in baskets around the room, or at tables so that students can preview them—one title per corner, basket, or table.
- Index cards/pieces of paper and pencils/pens to write Book Club Group choices

Before Reading

On the first day, begin the Guided Reading time by telling children that you have selected four of Cynthia Rylant's wonderful *Henry and Mudge* chapter books for them to read in Book Club Groups. If this is the first session using this format, you might talk about how grown-ups often read the same book and get together with friends to talk about the book.

One at a time, show the cover of each book and using only the cover, get children thinking about what will be in these books and what they might read. Then, tell children that they only have five days to spend on these books and they don't have enough time or copies of the books for each child to read all four. Each Book Club Group will read one book and then hear about the other three books.

During Reading

Next, hand each child an index card and ask her to write her name and the numbers 1, 2, and 3 on the card. Explain that you are going to give students 20 minutes to preview the books—five minutes for each book. Place all of the copies of each book in the four corners of the room, on four tables, in four baskets, etc. Randomly assign children to groups. Have group 1 go to the first set of books, group 2 go to the second set of books, and so on. Set a timer for five minutes and tell children that when the timer sounds, they must move to the next corner (table, basket, etc.) and the next set of books.

After Reading

When 20 minutes are up, have children return to their seats write their first, second, and third choices on the index cards. If they have trouble deciding between their first and second choices, tell them not to worry too much about the order of choices since you can't guarantee they will get their first choices or even their second choices. Explain by saying, "I want the groups to be about the same size, and I need to put groups together that will work well together. I promise I will give you one of your choices, and I will try to give you your first choices but I can't promise that!"

[Cynthia Rylant]

Purpose

To talk about chapter books and how to read them; for students to read the first chapter in their books, and learn the characters, setting, and Henry's problem

Before:	Talk about the characters and problem for each of the chapter books.
During:	Have students read the first chapters of their books to find characters and problems.
After:	Have each group list and tell the characters and problem for their book.

Preparation/Materials Needed

- Create and post a list of the groups based on the choices students wrote on their cards; indicate group leaders by marking with asterisks or highlighting.
- Student copies (five to seven) of the chosen books
- A Problem and Solution Chart (page 186) on chart paper and markers for each group

Before Reading

Talk about today's task. Each group will read the first chapter in their assigned book to find the characters, setting, and problem. Talk about how students will read a chapter a day with their Book Club Groups. Be sure to tell the groups that when they read chapter books they will try to remember what has happened so far and predict what will happen each time they read. Let them know that after reading today, their groups will discuss what has happened in the first chapters of their books. Then, they will record the information on Story Maps (page 185) so that they can share with the whole class after reading. Then, if there is time, they will think about and discuss what will happen in the chapters they will read tomorrow.

During Reading

Have students work together (echo reading, partner reading, or reading by themselves depending on the grade level and reading levels of students in your class) to read the first chapters to identify the characters, settings, and problems in their books. Monitor and coach the four Book Club Groups or one certain group that may need extra help in completing this task, noting and praising students as they remember characters, settings, and the problems in their *Henry and Mudge* books. Are some children having trouble reading the text? Are the leaders good "teachers," coaching those children to decode unknown words but not telling them the words they miss? See if students in the groups come up with good predictions for what might happen next. Do they need your help to do this? (The names of the second chapters may give the groups clues.)

After Reading

Meet as a whole class to share each group's Story Map that lists characters, setting, and problem for their *Henry and Mudge* book. If there is time, let all of the groups share what they think are their best predictions for what will happen in the next chapters of the books.

[Cynthia Rylant]

Purpose

For students to read the second chapter in their books to gain new information and think about three solutions

Before:	Have each group talk about the problem, the new information, and three possible solutions.
During:	Have groups read their second chapters and think of possible solutions to the problems.
After:	Have each group report on new information and three possible solutions.

Preparation/Materials Needed

- Student copies (five to seven) of the chosen books
- Problem and Solution Charts from Day 2
- Markers to add the three possible solutions to each chart

Before Reading

Remind the groups to first discuss what they learned yesterday. If this is the first time using Book Club Groups with chapter books for this class, you might use a chart from yesterday and discuss the characters, setting, and problem from one book. Then, suggest that each group leader give this quick review to the group before starting to read the second chapter. Remind the groups to talk about their predictions for today's reading. "What is the name of your next chapter? What do you think will happen in these chapters?" Remind the groups that during reading they will up with three possible solutions to each Henry's problems and list them on their charts.

During Reading

Instruct students to work together to read their second chapters (echo reading, partner reading, or reading by themselves depending on the grade level and reading levels of students in your class) Then, each group should discuss any new information they learned about the problem and come up with three possible solutions. Once again, monitor and coach the four Book Club Groups or one group that may need extra help in completing this task. Note and praise students as they read, discuss the new information, and come up with possible solutions.

After Reading

Meet back as a whole class to let students share their charts that list the three possible solutions to each problem in the four chosen books. Let them all of the groups also share the best predictions for what will happen in the chapters they will read next.

[Cynthia Rylant]

Purpose

For students to read the third chapter in their books and discard any solutions that don't seem possible now

Before:	Let students talk about the possible solutions and read to find if any need to be discarded.
During:	Have groups read their third chapters and discuss if any solutions need to be discarded.
After:	Have each group tell about new information and whether any solutions should be discarded.

Preparation/Materials Needed

- Student copies (five to seven) of the chosen books
- Problem and Solution Charts from Day 3
- Markers to cross out any solutions that don't seem possible now—or add any new solutions to the charts.

Before Reading

Remind the groups to first discuss where they are in their stories. Suggest that each group leader give a quick review to the group before starting to read the third chapter. The groups also need to talk about their predictions for today's reading. What is the name of this chapter? What do they think will happen in this chapter? Remind each group that during reading students will discuss if any of their three possible solutions to Henry's problem need to be crossed off the chart because of new information or if new solution(s) needs to be added.

During Reading

The students will work together (echo reading, partner reading, or reading by themselves depending on the grade level and reading levels of students in your class) to read the third chapters and then discuss any new information learned about the problems and whether it changes their lists of possible solutions. Once again, monitor and coach the four Book Club Groups or one certain group that may need extra help in completing this task, noting and praising students as they read.

After Reading

Meet as a whole class to share the groups' charts listing the three possible solutions to Henry's problem in each of the four chosen books. Let all of the groups share the best predictions for what will happen in the chapters they will read next.

[Cynthia Rylant]

Purpose

For students to read the fourth chapter in their books and discuss the solution to Henry's problem

Before:	Have students talk about the possible solutions and remind students to read to find the ending (solution).
During:	Have groups read their fourth and remaining chapters and discuss if the solutions were correct.
After:	Have each group share how their book about Henry and Mudge ended (the solution).

Preparation/Materials Needed

- Student copies (five to seven) of the chosen books
- Problem and Solution Charts from Day 4
- Markers to add the solutions found in the books

Before Reading

Remind the groups to first discuss where they are in their books. Suggest that each group leader give a quick review to the group before starting to read the fourth and final chapter(s).

The groups also need to talk about their predictions for today's reading. What is the name of this chapter? What do they think will happen in this chapter? Remind the groups that after reading they will discuss if any of their possible solutions were right and whether Henry's problems were solved in their books.

During Reading

Instruct students to work together (echo reading, partner reading, or reading by themselves depending on the grade level and reading levels of students in your class) to read their fourth and/or final chapter(s) and then discuss how Henry's problem was solved. Once again, monitor and coach the four Book Club Groups or one certain group that may need extra help in completing this task. Note and praise students as they read, discuss the new information in the final chapter(s), and come up with the solution to the problem in each of their *Henry and Mudge* books.

After Reading

Meet as a whole class to share each group's chart that lists the solution to Henry's problem in their book. Let all of the groups also share what they liked best about their books. If there is time, let children draw or write about their favorite parts of their books.

[Cynthia Rylant]

Extensions

Self-Selected Reading

- Read some of Cynthia Rylant's other books during your teacher read-aloud. Two especially wonderful books about family are *The Relatives Came* and *When I Was Young in the Mountains*.
- Encourage children to read books they did not read during Book Club Groups.

Writing

- Encourage students to write stories about boys (or girls) and dogs. Perhaps the stories could be based on their lives!
- Do an interactive mini-lesson and develop a chapter book with your class, writing one chapter per day for five days. Then, encourage children to write chapter books of their own.
- During a mini-lesson, write a book review (not a report but a review like you find in newspapers and magazines) of one of Cynthia Rylant's books.

Art

- Let children choose to draw Henry, Mudge, other favorite characters, or favorite parts of *Henry and Mudge* books after reading.
- Let children draw pictures from the *Henry and Mudge* books they like best. Are the pictures from the books they read or from one of the books another group reported on?

Guided Reading

- Complete a Story Map (page 185) for a Cynthia Rylant picture book or chapter book (one Story Map per chapter) that is read during Guided Reading.
- After reading, let children choose whether to draw or write about their favorite characters or parts of Cynthia Rylant books.

Working with Words

- Do a Making Words lesson with the word, **chapter**.
  Letters: a, e, c, h, p, r, t
  Make: at eat art car cat hat chat cart heat heap each cheap/peach chart cheat/teach reach preach chapter
  Sort: spelling patterns—-at, -art, -eat, -each
  Transfer: smart, tart, treat, beach
- If you read *When I Was Young in the Mountains*, do a Making Words lesson with the word, **mountain**.
  Letters: a, i, o, u, m, n, n, t
  Make: at am an man mat/tam tan/ant aunt/tuna atom into union mount amount nation mountain
  Sort: spelling patterns—-am, -an, -at, -ount
  Transfer: sham, slam, flat, Stan
- If you read *The Relatives Came*, do a Making Words lesson with the word, **relatives**.
  Letters: a, e, e, i, l, r, s, t, v,
  Make: at as set seal real steal trial vital easel reset relive reseal revise travel reveal several relatives
  Sort: spelling patterns—-eal; prefixes— re-
  Transfer: meal, steal, retold, reread

Book Club Groups to Teach Comprehension Strategies

The goal of the Guided Reading Block in Four-Blocks® classrooms is to teach comprehension. That is also the goal of reading when using the Book Club Groups format. Different types of literature require young children to master different comprehension skills and strategies. When people read stories, they need to follow the story structure and think about the characters, settings, events, and conclusions. Comprehension (understanding of the story) will be greater if the reader imagines herself in the situation the characters are in, predicts what characters will do, and evaluates the choices characters make based on what she thinks they should do. Readers will also comprehend better when they think about why things happen in a story and why characters behave in the way they do.

Even within fiction, there are differences in the specific comprehension strategies required. When reading mysteries, readers need to watch for clues and draw conclusions if they want the experience of solving the mystery before the author solves it for them. When reading fantasy, readers have to imagine a different world and infer the rules the characters in that world live by.

Informational reading requires different comprehension skills and strategies from fiction reading. In order to remember and learn from informational selections, readers have to figure out and remember the sequence in which specific events occurred even more than in stories. Events are often caused by previous events and readers need to think about what events cause other events, to happen. Often, several things—animals, people, events, places, etc.—are compared and contrasted. This requires the reader to summarize and draw conclusions about similarities and differences.

"...students need to use different comprehension skills and strategies."

[Comprehension Skills]

Poetry, plays, and directions each have their own structure. To understand these, students need to use different comprehension skills and strategies from those they use with stories and information. There are some comprehension strategies that need to be taught so that even young students can comprehend literally and inferentially.

After reading *Mosaic of Thought* by Ellin Keene and Susan Zimmerman (1997), many teachers became aware that comprehension needed to be taught and could be taught better. They were reminded in Keene and Zimmerman's book that:

1. Proficient readers spontaneously generate questions before, during, and after reading.

2. Proficient readers also ask questions to clarify the text or determine the author's purpose.

3. Proficient readers also know when a question needs to be answered and whether they can find the answer in the text or infer their answer from background knowledge and some clues in the text.

4. Proficient readers also understand how asking questions deepens their comprehension.

Keene and Zimmerman's work was expanded in Stephanie Harvey and Anne Goudvis's book *Strategies That Work* (2000), which tells teachers how to teach these mosaics of thought, and Debbie Miller's book *Reading with Meaning* (2002) in which she shares how she uses the strategies in her first-grade classroom. It is with these three books in mind that we wrote this chapter. Because Four-Blocks classrooms always read during Guided Reading time and do listening comprehension during the read-aloud portion of Self-Selected Reading, we have added "reading by students" to each Book Club Group lesson. Reading by students can be having students read with partners, read alone, or simply follow along with their eyes and fingers as the teacher reads a selection out loud the class.

The goal of the teacher during the Guided Reading Block is for all children to learn to comprehend or understand the text better. Some comprehension strategies in this chapter are: previewing and predicting making text-to-self or text-to-text connections, visualizing, inferring, and repairing understanding.

Strategy
Preview and Predict

When a teacher models previewing and predicting, and encourages students to preview and predict before reading, students become more engaged in the reading task and better understand what they are reading. The students' interest helps them have a purpose for reading. Good readers often preview the text before reading it. People do this when they pick up books at the bookstore, the library, off the rack in a store, or at an airport gift shop. In addition, good readers modify their predictions based on clues they find when reading the text. Even young students need to know that previewing and predicting is a good strategy to use when reading. When teaching these important reading strategies to students, you are going to introduce them to the whole class with an introductory text, often referred to in educational books as the anchor text. Next, you will have students use these strategies as they read text in small groups. Finally, you will encourage students to use the strategies as they read self-selected books on their own reading levels that are "just right" for them. The goal is for the strategies to become automatic for young readers and improve reading comprehension.

Suggested Preview and Predicting Books for Book Club Groups (choose four):
- *Click, Clack, Moo: Cows That Type* by Doreen Cronin (Simon and Schuster, 2000) GRL: K; RL: 1.3
- *Fireflies* by Julie Brinkloe (Scott Foresman, 1986) RL: 2.5
- *Fly Away Home* by Eve Bunting (Clarion Books, 1991) RL: 4.3
- *The Monster at the End of This Book* by Jon Stone (Random House, 2000) RL: 2.3
- *The Mysteries of Harris Burdick* by Chris Van Allsburg (Houghton Mifflin, 1984) RL: 3.5
- *Purple, Green and Yellow* by Robert Munsch (Annick Press, 1992) RL: 2.4
- *The Sweetest Fig* by Chris Van Allsburg (Houghton Mifflin, 1993) RL: 3.9
- *The Three Pigs* by David Weisner (Clarion Books, 2001) RL: 2.8
- *A Turkey for Thanksgiving* by Eve Bunting (Clarion Books, 1995) RL: 4.5
- *The Wednesday Surprise* by Eve Bunting (Clarion Books, 1989) RL: 2.9

Whole-Class Book for Day 1:
- *Suddenly!* by Colin McNaughton (Voyager Books, 1998) GRL: J; RL: 2.5
  This book will really entertain students as they try to predict what will happen to Preston the pig as the big, bad wolf stalks him throughout the day. The twists and turns of the plot keep the class guessing to the final page. (The book is available as a big book from HarperCollins Educational Books and in smaller, hardback and paperback versions.)

[Preview and Predict]

Purpose

To introduce the strategy of previewing a book and making predictions

Before:	Model previewing a book and making predictions as you read.
During:	Have students read the text, stopping after each "suddenly" to make a prediction.
After:	Discuss the surprises in this book and how and why students made the predictions.

Preparation/Materials Needed

- *Suddenly!* by Colin McNaughton

Before Reading

Bring in a book that you might read for pleasure and model for students how to browse through a book before buying it. Show them how you read the back cover, look inside the front cover, read a paragraph or two at the beginning, and maybe even "sneak a peek" at the ending to see what might happen. Let students know that previewing a text and predicting what might happen are strategies that good readers use before reading books.

Let children know that you will be helping them learn how to preview and predict as they read. Begin by showing the cover of the book *Suddenly!*, then ask students what they think the book is about. Tell students, "When I look at the cover of this book, I see a wolf and a pig. What I know about wolves and pigs tells me that this wolf may be looking for a nice lunch! I wonder why the title of the book is *Suddenly!*? I think

maybe the story will be scary and something will happen fast." Ask students to make predictions of what they think the story might be about. Do not show the illustrations inside this book before they read so that the students can make predictions as you read it together.

During Reading

You can read *Suddenly!* aloud to your class, having the students follow along with their eyes if you have the big book, or with their eyes and fingers if you have individual copies and teach first grade. Stop after each "Suddenly. . ." to allow students to predict what might happen. (If your students are in second or third grade, let them read the pages silently, stopping to make a prediction every time they get to the word, "suddenly.") List the predictions students are making on chart paper, the board, or a transparency as you read and come to "suddenly." Make sure you put a child's name next to each prediction. Make a two-column chart for the predictions that looks like this:

Prediction (Name)   Thinking Behind Prediction

Say something like, "Today, we will fill in the Prediction column. Each time I come to the word 'suddenly,' I will stop and ask you to predict what happens next." After reading and filling in the first column, discuss with students how predicting can keep their interest in the story, and add to the enjoyment and understanding of the of the text.

After Reading

After reading, discuss how the story was very different from what was expected. Discuss how the author changes the plot from what is a typical "wolf and pig" story to make it more

[Preview and Predict]

interesting and funny. Share how this relates to a good mystery that you might read. Say something like, "I always think that I have predicted the ending, but most of the time, the author surprises me. That is why I find mystery books so interesting. Predicting keeps

me interested in the story." Let students know that this is the purpose of predicting—not to be "right" but to make realistic guesses based on information the authors told them when they read the books.

Purpose

For students to discover the thinking (why) behind their predictions

Before:	Review previewing and predicting; talk about the "thinking" behind predictions.
During:	Have students reread the text, thinking about the reasons behind all of the predictions.
After:	Fill in the second column of the chart listing the thinking behind predictions.

Preparation/Materials Needed
- *Suddenly!* by Colin McNaughton
- Chart of predictions from Day 1

Before Reading

Review the concepts of previewing and predicting. Remind students that good readers preview and predict when reading, and that it can help keep them interested in the story and improve their understanding of a story (or reading comprehension). Tell students to think about their "thinking" and the reasons behind their predictions as you (or they) reread *Suddenly!*

During Reading

Read *Suddenly!* aloud to your students again, having them follow along if you have the books and teach first grade. (If you teach second or third grade, let them reread the book with partners or by themselves.) After children finish reading, have them think about the predictions they made each time they stopped at the word "suddenly." What was their thinking and reasons behind each prediction?

[Preview and Predict]

After Reading

Gather the children together and have them look at the chart of predictions from the first day. Stop after the first child's prediction. Ask the child for his thinking behind the prediction. What made him think that? Were there clues in the text? Was it from prior knowledge about similar stories? List these in the Thinking

Behind Prediction column of the chart. Reread the text to help students, if necessary. Was the prediction confirmed as you (or they) read on? If so, place a large "C" next to the prediction. Discuss how predicting kept students interested in the story and talk about the various sources students draw from to make their predictions.

Purpose

For students to preview the four books, make predictions about each book, and decide which books they would like to read

Before:	Preview the four books with the class; explain the Preview and Predict Form. (See page 187.)
During:	Have each child look at and read a page or two from each of the four books.
After:	Have children select the books they want to read and write their choices on index cards.

Preparation/Materials Needed

- A list of the children randomly assigned to four groups
- Student copies (five to seven) of the four books to be previewed are placed in the

four corners of the room, in baskets around the room, or at tables so that students can preview them—one title per corner, basket, or table.
- Copies of the Preview and Predict Form for each student (page 187) Students will also use the this form to list their book choices also.

Before Reading

On the first day, begin Guided Reading time by telling children that you have selected four wonderful books for them to read in Book Club Groups. Each selection is a good book for making predictions. One at a time, show the cover of each book and using only the cover, get children to predict what each book might be about and what they might read. Model how to fill out the Preview and Predict form by writing the name of the book, the author, and your predictions. Remind the class that some of them had different predictions and they will write their predictions in the space provided.

[Preview and Predict]

Have students follow this procedure with all four books.

Then, tell children that they only have two days to spend on these books and they don't have enough time or copies of the books for each child to read all four books. Tell children, "Each Book Club Group will read one book, making predictions and thinking about the reasons for those predictions. Then, we will all hear about the other three books. Today, your job is to look at all four books, make some predictions about the books, write them on the form, decide which books you want to read, and list your choices." Use their completed forms to help assign students to the Book Club Groups. Remember to choose a good leader for each group and match reading levels when possible.

During Reading
Give each child a Preview and Predict Form and ask him to write his name on it. Explain that you are going to give students 20 minutes to preview the books—five minutes for each book. Place all of the copies of each book in the four corners of the room, on four tables, in four baskets, etc. Randomly assign children to four groups. Have children in group one go to the first set of books,

children in group two go to the second set of books, and so on. Set a timer for five minutes (or use the classroom clock and a bell or buzzer) and tell children that when the bell rings (or the buzzer sounds), they must move to the next corner (table, basket, etc.) and the next group of books to begin previewing and filling out the forms.

After Reading
When the 20 minutes are up, have children return to their seats; look at their predictions; and write their first, second, and third choices on their Preview and Predict Forms. If students have trouble deciding between their first and second choices, tell them not to worry too much about the order of choices since you can't guarantee they will get their first choices or even their second choices. Say something like, "I want the groups to be about the same size, and I need to put students in groups that will work well together. I promise that I will give you one of your choices, and I will try to give you your first choices but I can't promise that! If you don't get your first choices you can always read them when they get put in the Self-Selected Reading baskets after Book Club Groups."

[Preview and Predict]

Purpose

For students to use background knowledge and text clues to preview and predict what will happen in each of the four stories

Before:	Map out the next two days, then review how to preview and predict when reading.
During:	Have each group read half of their book one page at a time and make some predictions.
After:	Have children talk about their predictions and the reasons behind them.

Preparation/Materials Needed

- Student copies (five to seven) of the chosen books
- Create and post a list of the groups based on the choices students wrote on their cards; indicate group leaders by marking with asterisks or highlighting.
- Two-column Prediction Chart on chart paper and markers for each group

Prediction (Name)   Thinking Behind Prediction

Before Reading

Meet with the entire class to map out the next two days of Guided Reading. Discuss how each group will meet together, where they will meet, how they will read (echo reading after the leader or with partners depending on the grade level and reading level of the children), and how much they will read (half of the text). Put a paper

clip in a good stopping place halfway through each book, since many children's books don't have page numbers. Give each group a copy of the two-column Prediction Chart. Remind children to refer to the class chart you did for the book *Suddenly!* for ideas on how to complete their charts. Remind each group to make at least one prediction (they will possibly come up with several predictions) while reading the first half the story. Then, they should talk about the reasons behind the predictions and write those on the chart.

During Reading

Have students work together in heterogeneous Book Club Groups to read the four selected stories (echo reading or partner reading depending on your class). As they read, have students list their predictions in the first columns, talk about the reasons behind those predictions, and then write the thinking behind the predictions on the charts in the second column. Monitor and coach the groups or work with one group that may need extra help. Walk around the room, "drop an ear" and listen, and praise students as they read and stop to make predictions. Listen to see that each group identifies the thinking and text clues behind their predictions. You may also make notations of children who need extra help so that you can work one-on-one with those students during Self-Selected Reading time.

After Reading

Have the class meet as a whole group to discuss the predictions they made during the reading of each of the four books. Give each Book Club

[Preview and Predict]

Group an opportunity to share their predictions with the other groups. Let each group determine if the leader or someone else selected by the group will share. (The person selected will also share the thinking behind the group's predictions.)

Purpose

For students to finish reading the four books and share new predictions that helped them better understand the stories

Before:	Talk about finishing up the books and about how making predictions helps.
During:	Have students finish reading (echo or partners) the four books with their Book Club Groups.
After:	Talk about any new predictions and understandings while finishing the books.

Preparation/Materials Needed

• Each group's two-column Prediction Chart from Day 4 and markers

Before Reading

Review the predictions each group made before reading on Day 4, and talk about whether the reading of the first half of the group's book has proven or unproven any of these predictions. Allow students to change predictions based on yesterday's reading. Remind them that, as they finish reading their books, they should use the prediction chart to record their predictions and the thinking behind their predictions. Also tell them that when they are finished reading, each group should come up with a short summary of their book, some predictions the group made while reading the second half, and the thinking (why) behind those predictions.

During Reading

Send students to groups to read as they did yesterday (echo reading or reading with partners). As they complete the reading, have students continue to list predictions on their groups' charts. Monitor and coach the groups, noting and praising students as they identify what prompted their predictions. As students complete their reading, have them review the predictions and draw pictures of their favorite or the most surprising parts of their groups' stories to share with the whole class.

[Preview and Predict]

After Reading

Gather all of the groups together. Have each group share a summary of their book and the chart that lists new predictions and the thinking behind the predictions. Post each group's completed charts for all to see. Let students have about 10 minutes to complete the illustrations of their favorite parts—these can be displayed with the charts, as well.

Extensions

Self-Selected Reading

- Take time to predict during teacher read-alouds in a variety of genres. Help students see this as a valuable strategy to build interest and improve comprehension. Suggest that they make predictions while reading Self-Selected Reading books.

Writing

- Encourage students to try to write an unpredictable story similar to Colin McNaughton's *Suddenly!* Discuss how twisting the plot can make for an interesting story. Model this during Writing mini-lessons with familiar fairy tales and other stories.

Guided Reading

- Research recommends the "gradual release of responsibility" to students (Pearson and Gallagher, 1983). One way to do this is to read a book to the whole class first and teach the strategy. Then, encourage students to make predictions in Book Club Groups and small group settings, and when reading by themselves.

Working with Words

- Do a Making Words lesson for the word, suddenly.
  Letters: e, u, d, d, l, n, s, y
  Make: den/Ned dens lens sun sudden suddenly
  Sort: beginning sounds—d, l; spelling patterns—-en; plurals
  Transfer: glad, fad, clay, plays

Strategy: Make Text-to-Self Connections

Research shows that using background knowledge and connecting new knowledge to prior knowledge can help improve comprehension (Tierney and Cunningham, 1984). Using schema (prior knowledge) is helpful to students at all grade levels. Many reading educators recommend the use of the proper terms with students. They say students, even young readers, can understand what terms mean and can use them correctly once they are explained and modeled for them. Introduce this important reading strategy to the whole class with an introductory or anchor text. Next, have children use this strategy as they read books in Book Club Groups. Finally, encourage students to use this strategy as they read books that are "just right" for them during Self-Selected Reading. (This lesson includes specific examples of the connections CeCe Tillman makes with her students when reading and talking about *Chrysanthemum*.)

Suggested Books for Book Club Groups on Making Text-to-Self Connections (choose four):

- *The Art Lesson* by Tomie dePaola (G. P. Putnam's Sons, 1989) GRL: M; RL: 2.5
- *Birthday Presents* by Cynthia Rylant (Orchard Books, 1991) GRL: K; RL: 2.8
- *Ira Sleeps Over* by Bernard Waber (Scott Foresman, 1975) GRL: L; RL: 3.5
- *Just Me and My Mom* by Mercer Mayer (Goldencraft, 1990) GRL: I; RL: 1.9
- *Little Critter's This Is My School* by Mercer Mayer (Goldencraft, 1990) GRL: K; RL: 2.5
- *My Great-Aunt Arizona* by Gloria Houston (HarperTrophy, 1997) GRL: L; RL: 3.5
- *Now One Foot, Now the Other* by Tomie dePaola (G. P. Putnam's Sons, 1980) GRL: L; RL: 2.5
- *Oliver Button Is a Sissy* by Tomie dePaola (Voyager, 1990) GRL: J; RL: 2.8
- *Roxaboxen* by Alice McLerran (Lothrop Lee and Shepard, 1991) GRL: M; RL: 4.3
- *The Snowy Day* by Ezra Jack Keats (Viking, 1981) GRL: J; RL: 3.2
- *When I Get Bigger* by Mercer Mayer (Golden Books, 1986) GRL: K; RL: 2.5

Whole-Class Book for Day 1:

- *Chrysanthemum* by Kevin Henkes (Greenwillow Books, 1991) GRL: L; RL: 4.2
  This book is about a little mouse who loves her name until she goes to school and her classmates make fun of her. She loses confidence until her music teacher helps her realize how special her name really is.

[Text-to-Self Connections]

Purpose

For students to make text-to-self connections

Before:	Discuss text-to-self connections and give an example of one for the children
During:	Read *Chrysanthemum* and have students think about how she felt about her name
After:	Discuss any text-to-self connections students had.

Preparation/Materials Needed

• *Chrysanthemum* by Kevin Henkes

Before Reading

On the first day, discuss what connections are, and how making connections with a story or a character in the story can help a reader better understand the story. If possible, bring in a chain and show how the links are connected to illustrate what connection means. Write the word schema, and explain how this is thinking about what you already know or using your background knowledge. Tell students that although there are many ways that readers use schema, today the focus will be text-to-self connections. Begin by showing the cover of *Chrysanthemum* and telling a little about what the book is about.

This is how CeCe might begin her "think-aloud" of connections. "When I was a little girl, my family called me 'Sissy.' I was perfectly happy with my name until I went to first grade. When my first-grade teacher called roll, she went down the list...' Julie, Rex, Donna, Cecilia.' When she said Cecilia, I remember looking around the room thinking, "Who is that???" I was so shocked to find out that this person was me!!! I was never so mortified in my life! When I read the book Chrysanthemum, I know just how she feels at school, because I felt the same way."

During Reading

Read *Chrysanthemum* aloud. If you have enough student copies, let children follow along with their eyes and fingers. Remind them of how connections help comprehension during reading. Later, as she gets to the part about the music teacher, this is how CeCe's think-aloud might sound: "When I see how the music teacher made Chrysanthemum feel about her name, I am reminded of my second-grade teacher, Miss Hardy. On the first day of school, she asked me my name. I said 'Cecilia' with my head down just like Chrysanthemum. Then, my teacher said 'Cecilia!! That's much too big a name for such a pretty little girl! How about we call you CeCe!' And, I have been CeCe to my friends ever since that day. I know just how Chrysanthemum felt about her music teacher because that is just how I feel about Miss Hardy!"

After Reading

Emphasizing the personal connection the story has for you really illustrates the concept of connections. Because this is an introductory or anchor text, continually refer back to it when reminding students about text-to-self connections. End this day's lesson with discussion of text-to-self connections the students may have about this book or another. Don't be discouraged if they seem unsure at first. You might prompt them to look for text-to-self connections during Self-Selected Reading time to share after reading.

[Text-to-Self Connections]

Purpose

For students to make text-to-self connections with *Chrysanthemum*

Before:	Review text-to-self connections and schema; remind students to use these as they read.
During:	Reread *Chrysanthemum* or have the students read in play school groups of five.
After:	Talk about text-to-self connections, and let students write or draw their connections.

Preparation/Materials Needed

- *Chrysanthemum* by Kevin Henkes
- One piece of chart paper for every five students
- Crayons, markers, or colorful pencils
- Self-stick notes
- One piece of chart paper that lists "play school" groups of five with asterisks for teachers (optional format for second or third grade)

Before Reading

Review the concepts of text-to-self connections and schema. Remind students how using schema and making connections can help a reader better comprehend text. Ask the readers to describe how the connections make them feel, and how they help them better understand the story or the characters in the story.

During Reading

Read *Chrysanthemum* aloud again to students (or use a "play school format"—groups of five with one student in each group playing the teacher—if students are second or third graders and most students can read the text). Encourage children to signal a connection (by lifting fingers, or showing thumbs-up). You (or the "teacher" in each group) should stop the reading to listen to their connections. Always bring it back to the text by asking (or having the group "teachers" ask) the child how it helps her better understand the story. This will encourage more meaningful connections. Never discourage children by implying "right" or "wrong" answers but point out those connections that are particularly helpful to understanding texts. Use self-stick notes to mark pages where you make text-to-self connections and let children share the connections with the class (or their groups, depending on the format). Walk around the room and monitor students' reading and connections if they are working in groups. Make note of any interesting connections and ask students to share them with the whole class after reading.

After Reading

Randomly assign students to groups of five (or use the "play school" groups if you are using that format). Give each group a piece of chart paper and seat students around the sides of the paper. Have students draw pictures or write about their connections with this story for 10 minutes. Then, let the groups share their connections with the whole class. Be sure to ask students with the particularly interesting connections you noted to share.

[Text-to-Self Connections]

Purpose
For students to preview the four books and decide which books they would like to read

Before:	Preview the four books with the class.
During:	Have each child look at and read a page or two from each of the four books.
After:	Have children select the books they want to read and write their choices on index cards.

Preparation/Materials Needed
- A list of children randomly assigned to four groups
- Student copies (five to seven) of the four books to be previewed are placed in the four corners of the room, in baskets around the room, or at tables so that students can preview them—one title per corner, basket, or table.
- Index cards/pieces of paper and pencils/pens to write Book Club Group choices

Before Reading
On the first day, begin the Guided Reading time by telling children that you have selected four wonderful books for them to read in Book Club Groups. One at a time, show the cover of each book and using only the cover, get children to predict what each book might be about and what they might read. Then, tell children that they only have two days to spend on these books and they don't have enough time or copies of the books for each child to read all four books. Each Book Club Group will read one book, make

text-to-self connections, and then hear about the other three books. Today, their job is to look at all four books and decide which books they want to read, which books they can read, and which books would be good for them to make text-to-self connections with while reading.

During Reading
Next, hand each child an index card and ask her to write her name and the numbers 1, 2, and 3 on the card. Explain that you are going to give students 20 minutes to preview the books—five minutes for each book. Places all of the copies of each book in the four corners of the room, on four tables, in four baskets, etc. Randomly assign children to groups. Have group one go to the first set of books, group two go to the second set of books, and so on. Set a timer for five minutes (or use the classroom clock and a bell or buzzer) and tell children that when the bell rings (or the buzzer sounds), they must move to the next corner (table, basket, etc.) and the next set of books.

After Reading
When the 20 minutes are up, have children return to their seats to write down their first, second, and third choices. When they have trouble deciding between first choice and second choices, tell the students not to worry too much about the order of choices. You can't guarantee they will get their first choices or even their second choices. Tell students, "I want the groups to be about the same size, and I need to put groups together that will work well together. I promise I will give you one of your choices, and I will try to give you your first choices but I can't promise that. But, remember all of the books will be available for everyone to read during self-selected reading after we finish with them."

[Text-to-Self Connections]

Purpose

For students to use background knowledge and identify text-to-self connections that helped them better understand the stories their Book Club Groups read

Before:	Review text-to-self connections; remind students to think about these when reading.
During:	Have students take turns reading half of the books, one page at a time, and talking about text-to-self connections.
After:	Have each group make a list of text-to-self connections they had when reading the book.

Preparation/Materials Needed

- Student copies (five to seven) of the chosen books
- Create and post a list of the groups based on the choices students wrote on their cards; indicate group leaders by marking with asterisks or highlighting.
- Four to five self-stick notes for each child
- Chart paper and markers for each group to list the connections made by group members

Before Reading

Meet with the entire class to map out the next two days of reading. Discuss how each group should meet together to read the first half of the book today and finish the book tomorrow. Explain how you have placed a paper clip at a good stopping place approximately halfway through each text. Today, have the groups read to the paper clips in their books. Explain that, one at a time, each student will read a page aloud to his group. Give each child a self-stick note to write his name and remind students to place them in the books where connections are made to the texts. Also, remind students to be ready to discuss how the connections helped them better understand their stories.

During Reading

Instruct students to work together to read half of their selected stories. Ask them to take turns reading a page aloud to their groups and identifying connections or asking for any connections other students might have. Ask the leaders to coach any students who are having trouble decoding or making connections. Your job is to rotate among the groups and help, if needed. Monitor and coach the groups, noting and praising students as they make connections. Make note of students who may need some one-on-one help during Self-Selected Reading time.

After Reading

Give students five minutes to share connections with students in their groups. Remind students to add their connections to the groups charts and allow them to do that during this time. Then, meet as a whole class, share the charts, and discuss the connections students in each group made during the reading of their book. Then, as a class, create a definition of text-to-self connection and schema to post with the charts.

[Text-to-Self Connections]

Purpose

For students to share the connections they have made during reading and how the connections helped them better understand the stories

Before:	Review some text-to-self connections.
During:	Have students finish reading their books and making text-to-self connections.
After:	Let students draw or write about the connections and how they helped them understand the story.

Preparation/Materials Needed

- Connections charts from Day 4
- Large chart or drawing paper for each group
- Markers, crayons, or colorful pencils
- Tape to post charts

Before Reading

Review the class definitions of text-to-self connection and schema. Discuss the purpose for reading these books. Allow a few children who have already made connections to share these with the class. Post a piece of unlined chart paper on the board. Model how each child will sit on one side of the chart paper to draw or write about her connections after finishing the book with her Book Club Group.

During Reading

Send students to groups to finish reading just as they read yesterday (taking turns reading aloud one page at a time). As groups complete the reading, have students discuss the connections they made and talked about yesterday. Monitor the groups and coach them as they complete the reading and begin talking about their connections. Make sure students understand that they will draw or write about their connections after reading.

After Reading

Let children use markers, crayons, or colorful crayons to draw or write about their connections on their groups' pieces of chart paper. Let each group have time to look at the work in progress on other groups' charts. Finally, allow time for a couple of students in each group to share their connections with the whole class.

[Text-to-Self Connections]

Extensions

Self-Selected Reading

- Share connections during read-alouds in a variety of genres. Begin to expand from text-to-self connections to text-to-text and text-to-world connections. Model each of these during think-alouds at Self-Selected Reading time.

  Here are some books that are especially good to read and make connections:

  Cynthia Rylant: *Birthday Presents* (Orchard Books, 1991), *The Relatives Came* (Antheneum, 2001), *When I Was Young in the Mountains* (E. P. Dutton, 1993)

  Patricia Polacco: *Chicken Sunday* (The Putnam & Grosset Group, 1992), *The Keeping Quilt* (Aladdin Paperbacks, 1988), *Mrs. Mack* (Philomel, 1998), *Some Birthday!* (Simon and Schuster, 1991), *Thank You, Mr. Falker* (Philomel, 1998)

  Judith Viorst: *Alexander and the Terrible, Horrible, No Good, Very Bad Day* (Aladdin Books, 1972)

  Kevin Henkes: *Julius: The Baby of the World* (Greenwillow Books, 1990), *Owen* (Greenwillow Books, 1993), *Sheila Ray, the Brave* (Mulberry Books, 1996)

  Arnold Lobel: *Days with Frog and Toad* (HarperTrophy, 1984), *Frog and Toad All Year* (HarperTrophy, 1984), *Frog and Toad Are Friends* (HarperTrophy, 1979), *Frog and Toad Together* (HarperTrophy, 1979)

Writing

- Encourage students to share connections during Writing time. During mini-lessons, model connections between texts and between life experiences and the subject matter in science and social studies during mini-lessons. This will give students encouragement to begin sharing their own connections.

Guided Reading

- Research recommends the "gradual release of responsibility" to students (Pearson and Gallagher, 1983). One way to do this is to teach text-to-self connection strategies to the whole class, then let children work on the same strategies in small groups. Finally, encourage students to use the strategies when reading by themselves at Self-Selected Reading time. Using the Text-to-Self Connections reproducible (page 188) will help students make connections until it becomes automatic when reading independently.

Working with Words

- Do a Making Words lesson with the name, **Chrysanthemum**.
  Letters: a, e, u, c, h, h, m, m, n, r, s, t, y
  Make: us as an ant/tan can the hen hem them then came same name anthem Chrysanthemum
  Sort: beginning sounds—th; spelling patterns—-an, -em, -en, -ame
  Transfer: plan, gem, pen, flame

[Text-to-Self Connections]

Other Suggestions

- Begin charting students' text-to-self connections. Let students add titles and their names to the chart as they make text-to-self connections during Self-Selected Reading and other reading times during the day. As students begin to internalize the language of connections and using it throughout the day, praise the connections they make.

Strategy 2

Question and Monitor

Good readers monitor text as they read, always making sure the text makes sense to them. As young readers develop, the need to question and monitor their reading is vital. Children need to learn to monitor their reading to ensure that the text makes sense. In addition, asking questions of both themselves and the author can help students navigate text with clearer understanding. When developing questioning strategies with students, use engaging fiction and nonfiction. Nonfiction can help awaken the children's natural curiosity about the world and how things work. When you teach this strategy, work with a whole-class text then in Book Club Groups. Finally, remind students to do use the strategy when they read "just right" books in Self-Selected Reading.

Suggested Question and Monitor Books for Book Club Groups (choose four):
- *All I See* by Cynthia Rylant (Orchard Books, 1988) GRL: M; RL: 4.9
- *The Butterfly Book* by Gail Gibbons (HarperTrophy, 1990) GRL: O; RL: 4.6
- *Fly Away Home* by Eve Bunting (Clarion Books, 1991) GRL: M; RL: 4.3
- *How Many Days to America?* by Eve Bunting (Clarion Books, 1990) GRL: S; RL: 3.2
- *Jumanji* by Chris Van Allsburg (Houghton Mifflin, 1980) GRL: M; RL: 4.4
- *Pink and Say* by Patricia Polacco (Philomel, 1994) GRL: S; RL: 4.9
- *Planet Earth, Inside Out* by Gail Gibbons (Mulberry Books, 1990) GRL: O; RL: 4.6
- *The Wednesday Surprise* by Eve Bunting (Clarion Books, 1989) GRL: K; RL: 2.9
- *Why Is the Sky Blue?* by Marian B. Jacobs (Rosen, 1998) GRL: M; RL: 4.5

Most of these books require very good second- or third-grade readers. The *Wednesday Surprise* is an easier selection, and *Pink and Say* is slightly harder and heavier than the other selections.

Whole-Class Book for Day 1:
- *The Stranger* by Chris Van Allsburg (Houghton Mifflin, 1986) RL: 3.5
  In this unusual tale, a man is hit by a truck and the man who is driving takes him home. The "stranger," the man who was hit, cannot remember who he is. Van Allsburg gives clues to help the reader discover the identity of the "stranger."

[Question and Monitor]

Purpose

To model how to use questioning strategies to uncover the identity of the "stranger" in the story

Before:	Model how sometimes we have questions before we read; list any questions.
During:	Read the book aloud to the class as they follow along; stop to list questions.
After:	Ask students if they have any questions after reading. List them if they do.

Preparation/Materials Needed

- *The Stranger* by Chris Van Allsburg
- Chart paper
- Three markers in different colors: one for questions before reading, one for questions during reading, and one for questions after reading
- A paper bag with objects hidden inside (or special treats for the class)

Before Reading

Bring to class a paper bag with one or two objects hidden inside. Tell students that you will give them a chance to guess what is in the bag. Explain that they must ask you questions to try to discover what is in the bag. Allow students to ask questions to gain clues about what is in the bag. When they guess correctly, show them the object. Repeat this with a second object. Discuss how good questions can help them discover the objects quickly. Next, show students the book *The Stranger* by Chris Van Allsburg. Let them choose one color of marker and use the marker to list any questions students may have before reading the book. Have them discuss the possible identity of the "stranger" in this story.

During Reading

Begin to read the book aloud to the class. If you have enough books, let students follow along with you as you read. Using a different marker color (see Before Reading above), record any questions students have as you read the text to them. Stop after each page to list questions students have. Read through half of the text using this procedure.

After Reading

Discuss the questions already asked and whether any of them were answered as you read today. If students answered questions, then write the answers beside the appropriate questions. Using a third marker color, make a list of any new questions students might have from today's reading. Discuss how asking questions helped everyone think and helped with the understanding, or comprehension, of the story. It is also important to help students understand that not all questions are answered in every story they read.

[Question and Monitor]

Purpose

To continue to work on the strategy that asking questions helps with the comprehension of a story and identify the stranger in this story

Before:	Review the questions students had before, during, and after reading.
During:	Continue to read the book aloud to students; continue listing any questions.
After:	If students have questions after reading, list those questions. Then, let students talk, draw, and write about their favorite parts.

Preparation/Materials Needed

- *The Stranger* by Chris Van Allsburg
- Chart paper
- Three markers in different colors: one for questions before reading, one for questions during reading, and one for questions after reading
- A 9" x 12" (23 cm x 30 cm) piece of newsprint for each child
- Markers, crayons, and colorful pencils for drawing

Before Reading

Review the questions from the day before. Discuss any further questions the students may have thought of since yesterday. Use the same marker color as yesterday's before to record these questions.

During Reading

Continue reading *The Stranger* to the children, stopping if the students have further questions. List these questions in the same marker color as the during color from the day before. Have the students continue to try to figure out who the stranger is from the clues given in the story.

After Reading

List any final questions in the same marker color as the after reading questions from the day before. Discuss any questions that were answered in today's reading and list their answers next to the questions on the chart paper. Discuss those questions that were not answered, and where or if students can find the answers somewhere else. Talk about the "stranger." Let several children tell about their favorite parts of the book. Then, let each child write a sentence about his favorite part of this book and illustrate it with a picture.

[Question and Monitor]

Purpose

For students to preview the four books and decide which books they would like to read

Before:	Preview the four books with the class.
During:	Have each child look at and read a page or two from each of the four books.
After:	Have children select the books they want to read and write their choices on index cards.

Preparation/Materials Needed

- A list of children randomly assigned to four groups
- Student copies (five to seven) of the four books to be previewed are placed in the four corners of the room, in baskets around the room, or at tables so that students can preview them—one title per corner, basket, or table.
- Index cards/pieces of paper and pencils/pens to write Book Club Group choices

Before Reading

On the first day, begin Guided Reading time by telling children that you have selected four interesting books for them to read in Book Club Groups. One at a time, show the cover of each book and using only the cover, get children to ask some questions about each book. ("What might this book be about?") Then, tell children that they only have two days to spend on these books and they don't have enough time or copies of the books for each child to read all four books. Each Book Club Group will be reading one book, asking questions about that book, and reading to find the answers to those questions. They will all hear about the other three books that they do not read. Today, their job is to look at all four books, ask some questions about each of the books, and then decide which books they want to read.

During Reading

Next, hand each child an index card and ask him to write his name and the number 1, 2, and 3 on the card. Explain that you are going to give students 20 minutes to preview the books—five minutes for each book. Place all of the copies of each book in the four corners of the room, on four tables, in four baskets, etc. Randomly assign children to groups. Have children in group one go to the first set of books, children in group two go to the second set of books, and so on. Set a timer for five minutes (or use the classroom clock and a bell or buzzer) and tell the children that when the bell rings (or buzzer sounds), they must move to the next corner (table, basket, etc.) and the next group of books.

After Reading

When the 20 minutes are up, have children return to their seats to write their first, second, and third choices on the index cards. Collect the cards and use them to make your Book Club Groups. Place children in appropriate groups, honoring the book selections that most closely match their reading levels.

[Question and Monitor]

Purpose

To use questioning as a strategy to help students monitor their comprehension and read text more effectively

Before:	Talk about the importance of questioning when reading and what students will read.
During:	Have students begin reading the books with their Book Club Groups.
After:	Discuss each group's questions and if they have found any answers.

Preparation/Materials Needed

- Student copies (five to seven) of the chosen books
- Create and post a list of the groups based on the choices students wrote on their cards; indicate group leaders by marking with asterisks or highlighting.
- Self-stick notes for each group
- Chart paper and markers for each group

Before Reading

Meet with the entire class to map out the next two days of reading. Discuss how each group should meet together, where they should meet, and how they will read their book (take turns reading aloud one page at a time or partner reading). Give each group a set of self-stick notes to record questions in the text, and chart paper to list the questions. They can either post the self-stick notes on the chart or have a scribe rewrite the questions.

During Reading

Have students work together to read selected stories and list their questions on self-stick notes. Monitor and coach the groups, noting and praising students as they list questions that demonstrate they are thinking deeply about the text.

After Reading

Meet as a whole class to discuss the stories and questions asked during the stories. Have each group report to the whole class. Discuss with students whether their questions can be answered by looking for clues in the texts (T), by inferring (I), and/or by using outside sources (OS). Help the groups code their charts according to their ideas. Students will refer to their groups' charts during tomorrow's reading.

[Question and Monitor]

Purpose

For students to continue to read and list questions, or reread as needed to infer and find answers to questions

Before:	Go over the questions and students' coding from yesterday.
During:	Have students reread the text to see if they found the answers as coded.
After:	Discuss the answers and where they found them.

Preparation/Materials Needed

- Student copies (five to seven) of the chosen books
- Self-stick notes for each group
- Chart paper and markers for each group to record questions

Before Reading

Review the class charts from the day before, reminding students that they are going to continue to read and ask questions. Today, they will code their own questions according to the following key.

(T) if a question can be answered by looking for clues in the text

(I) if a question can be answered by inferring from the author's words

(OS) if a question must be answered from other sources

Encourage students to reread as necessary to find answers to the (T) and (I) questions.

During Reading

Send students to read in their groups. As they complete their reading, have them reread, if necessary, to find the answers to the questions they have generated. For those questions that must be answered from other sources, have students brainstorm which sources they think may have the answers. If possible, allow them to visit the library or use the Internet to find other sources to answer their questions. Monitor the groups and coach them as students complete the reading and begin to find answers to their questions.

After Reading

Let each group have time to look at the work in progress on other groups' charts. Allow time for each group to share their questions and where they found the answers, if they have found them. Discuss questions students may have had that were unanswered by the text. As a culminating activity, brainstorm with students why readers ask questions. Focus on how this strategy can help them be better readers.

[Question and Monitor]

Extensions

Self-Selected Reading

- Take time to allow students to ask questions during read-alouds. Model questioning during think-alouds in Self-Selected Reading. Help students see this as a valuable strategy to build interest and improve comprehension.

Writing

- Give students opportunities to use their journals as "Wonder Books." Let each student use journal pages to write questions she may wonder about. Then, let her choose one of the questions and do some research to find the answer. This is a great way to do short, focused research projects in the primary grades.

Guided Reading

- Research recommends the "gradual release of responsibility" to students (Pearson and Gallagher, 1983). One way to do this is to encourage students to use Questioning Webs (page 189) to list questions and then brainstorm about answers to the questions. Students can use copies of the reproducible form (page 189) when reading in small groups or individually.

Working with Words

- Do a Making Words lesson with the word, **strangers**.
  Letters: a, e, g, n, r, r, s, s, t
  Make: an at sat rat/art/tar star seat neat near tear range stare stage strange strangers
  Sort: spelling patterns—-at, -ar, -eat, -ear, -ange
  Transfer: scar, meat, clear, change

Strategy
Summarize and Conclude

An important skill for young readers to develop is the ability to summarize what they are reading and to draw conclusions by using what the author says and the prior knowledge they bring to the story. Using fairy tales and other familiar stories can help some young readers learn this strategy without struggling through the text. Their total effort can be on summarizing and drawing conclusions rather than figuring out the story. Using a Story Map gives readers a visual aid to guide them as they break down the story. Retelling, acting out, or "doing the book" are demonstrations of summarizing. If students can accomplish these things after reading, you know that they truly understand or comprehend what they have read. Again, with this strategy, you will work with the whole group then with Book Club Groups. Finally, encourage students to do this when they read their own Self-Selected Reading books.

Suggested Summarize and Conclude Books for Book Club Groups (choose four):
- *Arthur's Computer Disaster* by Marc Brown (Little, Brown and Co., 1997) GRL: L; RL: 2.2
- *Click, Clack, Moo: Cows That Type* by Doreen Cronin (Simon and Schuster, 2000) GRL: K; RL: 1.3
- *Fly Away Home* by Eve Bunting (Clarion Books, 1991) GRL: M; RL: 4.3
- *How Many Days to America?* by Eve Bunting (Clarion Books, 1990) GRL: J; RL: 2.8
- *Just Plain Fancy* by Patricia Polacco (Dragonfly Books, 1990) GRL: O; RL: 3.8
- *The Keeping Quilt* by Patricia Polacco (Aladdin Paperbacks, 1988) GRL: M; RL: 5.3
- *Lilly's Purple Plastic Purse* by Kevin Henkes (Greenwillow Books, 1996) GRL: H; RL: 2.1
- *The Monster at the End of This Book* by Jon Stone (Random House, 2000) GRL: H; RL: 2.3
- *My Rotten Redheaded Older Brother* by Patricia Polacco (Aladdin Paperbacks, 1994) GRL: M; RL: 3.9
- *Oliver Button Is a Sissy* by Tomie dePaola (Voyager, 1990) GRL: J; RL: 2.8
- *Strega Nona* by Tomie dePaola (Scholastic, Inc., 1975) GRL: M; RL: 4.4
- *A Weekend with Wendell* by Kevin Henkes (Mulberry Books, 1995) GRL: K; RL: 3.1

You can use just about any picture book that is fiction (a story) and can be read by most of your students. We suggest picture books for this activity rather than chapter books because sometimes each chapter is a separate story (like the *Frog and Toad* books by Arnold Lobel). You will need to have five to seven copies of the four chosen books in your classroom, or you can borrow from another teacher, as many teachers do.

Whole-Class Book for Day 1:
- *The Three Little Pigs* (any version)
  Using the familiar folktale will give children an opportunity to practice the skill of summarizing.

[Summarize and Conclude]

Purpose

For students to learn how to use a Story Map to summarize a story and use the information to draw conclusions

Before:	Talk about a summary.
During:	Have students read *The Three Little Pigs* with partners and summarize it using Story Maps. (If you have a big book, use the shared reading format.)
After:	Discuss what happened in the book and students' Story Maps; write a summary together.

Preparation/Materials Needed

- *The Three Little Pigs* (any version, enough copies for partner reading or a big book version for shared reading)
- A Story Map (page 185) on paper for each set of partners
- Markers

Before Reading

Discuss the parts of a Story Map—the characters, setting, and what happened in the book (beginning, middle, end of the story). Discuss how most fiction (stories) follows this same basic format. Tell students that they will be reading a familiar story today, *The Three Little Pigs*, with partners. Next, they will use the Story Maps to summarize the story with their partners. Assign partners, tell the partners where they will read, and review the rules for partner reading, if needed. Tell them to pay attention, as they read, to the items on the Story Maps so that they can fill them in with their partners when they finish reading. (If you have a big book of this story, you can do a shared reading and shared writing of the Story Map with the class.)

During Reading

Have children read *The Three Little Pigs* with their partners. Each child will take a turn reading a page until the story is complete. As they read, walk around the class, "drop an ear," and listen. Make notes, in your mind or on paper, of who is reading and how she is reading. Help any partners that need help. When the partners finish reading, they should begin filling in the Story Maps.

If you are using a big book, use the shared reading format—reading the book with the children and letting them chime in on the parts they know. (Many children will chant, "Not by the hair of my chinny, chin, chin!")

After Reading

After reading, discuss how the story is organized and complete the Story Maps together, listing the title, author, setting, beginning, middle, and end of the story (or problem and solution). Ask students to help you write a statement to summarize the story. If they have trouble with this, try this idea that many teachers have used successfully. Draw 15 blanks on the board. Then, tell students that you will work together to find 15 words that tell what the story is about. Begin with the first part of the book and gradually move through the story, reviewing words, deleting words, and condensing as necessary to get 15 words that summarize the story.

[Summarize and Conclude]

Purpose

For students to preview the four books and decide which books they would like to read

Before:	Preview and give a book talk about each of the four books with the class.
During:	Have each child look at and read a page or two from each of the four books.
After:	Have children select the books they want to read and write their choices on index cards.

Preparation/Materials Needed

- A list of children randomly assigned to four groups
- Student copies (five to seven) of the four books to be previewed are placed in the four corners of the room, in baskets around the room, or at tables so that students can preview them—one title per corner, basket, or table.
- Index cards/pieces of paper and pencils/pens to write Book Club Group choices

Before Reading

On the first day, begin Guided Reading time by telling children that you have selected four books for them to read in Book Club Groups. Each book has a good story that they will be asked to summarize after reading. One at a time, show the cover of each book and using only the cover, get children to predict what each book might be about and what they might read about. Then, tell children that they only have two days to spend on these books, and they don't have enough time or copies of the books for each child to read all four books. Each Book Club Group will read one book, fill in a Story Map, summarize their book, and then tell the other groups about the book. Today, their job is to look at all four books, make some predictions about the books, and decide what books they want to read.

During Reading

Hand each child an index card and ask her to write her name and the numbers 1, 2, and 3 on the card. Explain that you are going to give students 20 minutes to preview the books—five minutes for each book. Place all of the copies of each book in the four corners of the room, on four tables, in four baskets, etc. Randomly assign children to groups. Have children in group one go to the first set of books, children in group two go to the second set of books, and so on. Set a timer for five minutes (or use the classroom clock and a bell or buzzer) and tell children that when the bell rings (or the buzzer sounds), they must move to the next corner (table, basket, etc.) and the next set of books.

After Reading

When 20 minutes are up, have children return to their seats to write down their first, second, and third choices on their index cards. Collect the cards and use them to make your Book Club Groups. Place children in appropriate groups, honoring the selections that most closely match their reading levels. Remind children that if they don't get their first choices, they can always read the books when they get put in the Self-Selected Reading baskets after Book Club Groups.

[Summarize and Conclude]

Purpose
For students to read books with groups and fill out Story Maps

Before:	Talk about how Story Maps help with summaries.
During:	Have groups read their books and begin to discuss them (echo, partner, or one page at a time).
After:	Have each group fill out a Story Map for their book.

Preparation/Materials Needed
- Student copies (five to seven) of the chosen books
- Create and post a list of the groups based on the choices students wrote on their cards; indicate group leaders by marking with asterisks or highlighting.
- A Story Map (page 185) on a chart or transparency for each group

Before Reading
Meet with the entire class to map out the next two days of reading. Discuss how each Book Club Group should meet together to read the text. Give each group a copy of a Story Map on chart paper. Remind students of the Story Map they did for *The Three Little Pigs*. They can refer to that Story Map as a model for how to complete the maps for the books they read today with their Book Club Groups.

During Reading
Have students work together to read the selected stories. Tell them to echo read, partner read, or take turns reading pages aloud to their groups. How they read these books depends on the text, the grade level of your students, and the time of year. Walk around the room as students read and work together to fill out their Story Maps. Monitor and coach the groups as needed, noting and praising students who are reading fluently and for Story Maps are easy tasks. These students are good candidates to lead Book Club Groups at other times.

After Reading
Instruct groups to discuss the stories they have read and to fill in their Story Maps. Give students 10 minutes, then let each group share their book and Story Map with the whole class.

[Summarize and Conclude]

Purpose

For students to practice writing brief summaries of the stories they read

Before:	Review the stories quickly with the four Story Maps; talk about a summary.
During:	Have groups reread their books, check the Story Maps, and begin to think of summaries.
After:	Have each group write a summary of their book.

Preparation/Materials Needed

- Story Maps from Day 3
- One piece of lined chart paper or a transparency for each group
- Markers, crayons, or colorful pencils

Before Reading

Review each Book Club Group's Story Map from yesterday. Talk about a summary and remind children of the summary you did for *The Three Little Pigs*. Give each group a large piece of lined chart paper or a transparency to write on. Discuss how each student needs to help his group come up with a brief summary. If you think that this will be a hard task, then you might need to draw 15 word-sized blanks on the chart papers or transparencies to help students complete the task. Let them know that it is all right to add, delete, or change words to make the summaries better. They will share their completed summaries in the after-reading phase of today's lesson.

During Reading

Send students to reread the books in their groups and to begin to discuss writing their summaries. They can reread the books as they did yesterday (echo, partner, or taking turns reading a page each), or each child can read her group's book alone, silently with her group. Rereading helps fluency, and some children who might have had problems yesterday may be able to read the books today. As they complete their reading, have students look at their groups' Story Maps, and then begin to discuss writing summaries. Walk among the groups, monitoring and coaching them as they complete the reading and begin to talk about their summaries.

After Reading

Let each group work on their summary for about 10 minutes, leaving time to look at the work in progress on other groups' summaries. Allow time for each Book Club Group to share their summary with the class. (For a handwriting lesson, you might have students copy their groups' summaries in their best handwriting.)

[Summarize and Conclude]

Extensions

Self-Selected Reading

- Take time to talk about or give a summary of the book you are using for your teacher read-aloud each day. Be sure to use a variety of genres. Help students see that summarizing is a valuable strategy to improve comprehension and one that students will be asked to do throughout their schooling.
- After a teacher read-aloud, ask a student to give you a brief summary of the book. In the primary grades, we might call this a "retelling" of the story.
- Remind first graders that when they cannot read a book, they can always use the pictures to "tell" the story.

Writing

- Model writing a summary during a Writing mini-lesson. Use familiar folktales or fairy tales, as well as other stories you have recently read to the class.
- Do some interactive writing with summaries, giving students the opportunity to help you as you write.
- Encourage students to write summaries during Self-Selected Reading and focused Writing mini-lessons. Writing a good summary is an important skill that they will be asked to do throughout their schooling.

Guided Reading

- Research recommends the "gradual release of responsibility" to students (Pearson and Gallagher, 1983). One way to do this is to teach a strategy, like summarizing, with a whole-class lesson, then review it with small groups of children helping each other. (We use the Book Club Groups format.) Finally, encourage students to write summaries on their own about things they are reading about.
- Writing a summary of a story, as a group or individually, is an appropriate after-reading activity.

Other Suggestions

- Writing summaries, in groups or individually, can and should be part of an after-reading activity for science or social studies, too. Writing connected to any kind of reading helps students comprehend better.

Book Club Groups for Social Studies and Science

> "...they read to learn with excitement and enthusiasm with trade books."

In elementary school, the curriculum is usually divided into subject areas, such as reading, language arts, mathematics, science, and social studies. Children are often taught these subjects at different times in the school day, but they must learn to integrate them to make sense of the world. Nonfiction (or informational) books are distinguished from fiction by their emphasis. Both may tell stories, and both may include facts. But in fiction, a story is uppermost, with facts sometimes used to support it; while in nonfiction, the facts are uppermost, with storytelling used as an expressive technique. Most classroom and school libraries contain more fiction than nonfiction (Duke and Bennett-Armistead, 2004).

Children read to learn at school in their assigned social studies or science books and while doing homework, but they read to learn with excitement and enthusiasm with trade books. Students learn about what men and women did in the past in their social studies textbooks, but biographies give far more intimate and revealing pictures of these people and their work. Textbooks may barely mention that birds seem to know when to migrate, but informational book authors like Seymour Simon probe the phenomena thoroughly and awaken the interest of young scientists.

Narrative text includes characters, setting, and plot (beginning, middle, and how the story ends), which are concepts we have emphasized in the author studies and while explaining comprehension strategies. Expository texts (informational books) are organized differently and require different skills and strategies while reading. An expository text "explains" or tells about something or someone. The ideas in informational books may be

[Social Studies and Science]

organized by sequence, listings or descriptions, comparison-contrast, cause-effect, or problem solving. Students must understand how the text is structured, as well as be able to read the words in the text. With Book Club Groups, teachers can read "just right" text written about the topics they are teaching in social studies and science. This is one way teachers can help students learn how to read informational books and be better prepared to navigate social studies and science textbooks both in their classrooms and later in life.

In the next two sections, we will explain Book Club Groups in the content areas. The first section features books on social studies topics, and is followed by a section with books on science topics. It is our goal to help children learn to read these books more critically and thus help them comprehend these texts and other informational texts better.

For Book Club Groups, you will often begin with a whole-class lesson to introduce a theme, a strategy (webbing, KWL, etc.), or text features. Then, you will work in small Book Club Groups to let children read informational books or stories. Finally, you will encourage children to use these strategies when reading independently. Your conversations during Self-Selected Reading conferences can check these strategies.

Social Studies Topic: Families and Grandparents

Grandma, Grandpa, Nana, Pappy, Babushka, Memere, Pepe, Granny, Poppa—no matter what they are called, grandparents have special relationships with children and are important parts of families. When studying families with your class, these books will provide a chance for children to connect and compare their grandparents with those presented in the books. Often teachers introduce a new theme, such as families, with a teacher read-aloud, then will have students read books about grandparents for Book Club Groups. There are so many books on families that the choices are endless. This is just one book that you could use to introduce a family theme to your class.

Whole-Class Book for a Teacher Read-Aloud before Book Club Groups:
- *The Wednesday Surprise* by Eve Bunting (Clarion Books, 1989) GRL: K; RL: 2.9
  It's Wednesday! Each Wednesday, Anna's grandmother comes to her house. Anna and her grandmother are working on something special on Wednesdays. They are preparing a surprise for the family—something to do with books. Anna is teaching her grandmother how to read. At the end, Grandmother surprises everyone on Dad's birthday by reading for the whole family.

Suggested Families and Grandparents Books for Book Club Groups (choose four):
- *The Baby Sister* by Tomie dePaola (Penguin Putnam Books, 1996) GRL: K; RL: 2.2
- *Chicken Sunday* by Patricia Polacco (The Putnam & Grosset Group, 1992) GRL: M; RL: 4.8
- *Families* by Ann Morris (Steck-Vaughn, 2001) GRL: E; RL: 1.5
- *Grandpa's Face* by Eloise Greenfield (The Putnam & Grosset Group, 1996) GRL: Q; RL: 3.8
- *Just Grandma and Me* by Mercer Mayer (Golden Books, 1985) GRL: I; RL: 2.3
- *Just Grandpa and Me* by Mercer Mayer (Golden Books, 2001) GRL: G; RL: 1.7
- *Nana Upstairs, Nana Downstairs* by Tomie dePaola (Penguin Putnam Books, 1973) GRL: L; RL: 3.7
- *Now One Foot, Now the Other* by Tomie dePaola (G. P. Putnam's Sons, 1980) GRL: L; RL: 2.5
- *Rechenka's Eggs* by Patricia Polacco (Penguin Putnam Books for Young Readers, 1996) GRL: M; RL: 3.5
- *Song and Dance Man* by Karen Ackerman (Knopf, 1988) GRL: O; RL: 3.8
- *Thunder Cake* by Patricia Polacco (The Putnam & Grosset Group, 1997) GRL: M; RL: 3.5

[Families and Grandparents]

Purpose

For students to preview and select possible Book Club Groups books and make predictions about each book

Before:	Model how to preview books.
During:	Have each child look at and read a page or two from each book, then write a prediction.
After:	Have children select the books they want to read and write their choices on forms.

Preparation/Materials Needed

- Student copies (five to seven) of the four books to be previewed are placed in the four corners of the room, in baskets around the room, or at tables so that students can preview them—one title per corner, basket, or table.
- A fiction book for modeling previewing
- A list of children randomly assigned to four groups
- Index cards/pieces of paper and pencils/pens to write Book Club Group choices
- A Preview and Predict Form (page 187) for each child

Before Reading

Tell students, "Today you are going to preview four books and make choices for Book Club Groups. Each of you will have a chance to preview all four books. Readers often preview books that they think might be of interest to them. They may even make predictions about the books or stories. A prediction may cause a good reader to want to read a book, or it may result in the reader deciding to look for another book to read. Today, as you look at the four books, I want you to make a prediction about each book as you decide which books you may want to read."

Pick up the copy of the fiction book you have selected and say, "Before you begin looking at the books, I'd like to model for you how I select a book. Recently, I selected this book from the bookstore (or library). When I first saw it, I looked at the cover, and it caught my interest. It was written by one of my favorite authors. I immediately started making some predictions using the title. After a moment or two, I opened to the first pages and began to read, and I predicted . . . ." Continue by describing your prediction and tell why the prediction helped you decide to read the book.

During Reading

Tell students, "Today, you will move from table to table to preview each of our Book Club Group selections. You will have five minutes to preview each book, make a prediction about what the book will be about, quietly discuss your predictions with your groups, and write your predictions on the form. Then, at my signal you will move to another table and start the preview and prediction work over again. All of these books are about grandparents, so look at the cover, title, and pictures, and think about what is happening with the grandparents and which books you would like to read. Make sure you read a page or two so that you will also be able to tell if you **can** read the books." Once the groups are in their places, walk around the room and monitor the groups, seeing that they are following directions. Remember to praise students for their excellent reading, good predictions, and quiet discussions.

[Families and Grandparents]

After Reading

Have students write their book choices next to the numbers 1, 2, and 3 at the bottoms of their Book Club Preview and Prediction forms. Give students a few minutes to discuss why they

made their choices with other members of their groups. Use these forms to help place students in Book Club Groups. Assign each group a leader who can read the text fluently, and if needed, can help other children in the group.

Purpose

For students to read the books and use the illustrations to retell the stories

Before:	Model how to use the pictures in a book to retell the story.
During:	Have groups chorally read using whisper voices.
After:	Let students retell the stories using the pictures in the books.

Preparation/Materials Needed

- Create and post a list of the groups based on the choices students wrote on their cards; indicate group leaders by marking with asterisks or highlighting.
- Student copies (five to seven) of the chosen books

Before Reading

Tell students, "Today, we are going to begin Book Club Groups. Our job today is to read our

stories and then use the illustrations to retell them to the other groups who have not read the stories. I'd like to model this for you using *The Wednesday Surprise*, a book I read to you yesterday (or before) during my teacher read-aloud."

Open the book and begin retelling the story using the illustrations. Pause for a moment, looking at the picture on page 4, then say, "This is Grandma. She is going to her granddaughter's house." Turn to page 7 and say, "This is Anna, and she is waiting for her grandmother."

On the next page, pause for a moment and ask, "Would someone like to retell the story on this page." Allow students to continue retelling the story using the illustrations on each page. Occasionally, provide one of your own retellings.

During Reading

Direct students by saying, "You are going to start Book Club Groups. When you meet, I want each group to chorally read your book together using your whisper voices. You should

[Families and Grandparents]

practice retelling the story using the illustrations when you finish reading. You should take turns retelling parts of the story. No person should tell the story for more than two pages in a row. The leader, or teacher, in each group will decide how many pages each person can read so that everyone in the group has a turn." Monitor and coach the groups. Make sure you praise students for their excellent whisper reading, retelling, or cooperative work. Also, make sure that each

group is ready to have someone retell their story to the other groups for the after-reading activity.

After Reading

Tell students, "Now, each of the four groups will share their book and retell their story using the illustrations in the book to guide them." Call on each group to do this. When all four groups finish, talk about what is alike in the books—a grandparent. Talk about what is different—what happened with the grandparents.

Purpose

For students to reread the books and make text-to-self connections about grandparents

Before:	Review text-to-self connections. (See page 93.) Remind the children how to use these as they read.
During:	Have students take turns rereading their books one page at a time and talk about text-to-self connections.
After:	Talk about text-to-self connections and let students write the important ones on charts to share with the class.

Preparation/Materials Needed

- A copy of *The Wednesday Surprise*
- Student copies (five to seven) of the chosen books
- Chart paper and black markers for each group

Before Reading

Tell students, "Today, I want you to reread your books with your Book Club Groups and make text-to-self connections while you read. I will model this for you using the book, *The Wednesday Surprise*." Read a few pages of the book, then think aloud and talk about how you remember a grandparent that visited you. "My grandmother would take the bus to our house and we ate lunch together. I always looked forward to it. Remembering how I looked

[Families and Grandparents]

forward to my grandmother's visits helps me understand how Anna felt in the book, *The Wednesday Surprise*." Then, say, "Because you are reading so many different books about grandparents, today is a good time for you to think-aloud, talk about, and write down any connections you made when reading books about grandparents."

During Reading

Before students go to the groups to read, talk about how they will read today. "Yesterday, you chorally read *The Wednesday Surprise*. Today, I want you to take turns reading one page at a time. When each group member finishes a page, he will stop and tell whether the text helps him remember something similar. Be sure to let other students share if the text brings back some memories for them. Whenever you make a connection, make sure you also tell how your connection improved your understanding of the book you are reading. When you are finished, your group may record some of the most important connections you made. Write your connections on the piece of chart paper so that you can share them with class after reading." Walk around the room, "dropping an ear" and listening to the children reread their books. Rereading should help some of them with fluency. Monitor and coach students' reading and their text-to-self connections as you rotate among the groups. Remind children to write important connections on their charts to share when the whole class gets back together.

After Reading

Have a student in each of the Book Club Groups share with the class the chart of connections her group members made while reading the book about grandparents. Let her share how these connections helped her group understand the story in their book. Share any connections between texts; these are called text-to-text connections.

[Families and Grandparents]

Extensions

Self-Selected Reading

- Take time to predict and share text-to-self and text-to-text connections during your read-aloud books in a variety of genres. Help students see this as a valuable strategy to improve comprehension. Suggest that they make predictions when reading self-selected books.

Writing

- Encourage students to write about text-to-self connections in self-selected writing. Model this during your writing mini-lessons by writing about a memory of a grandparent similar to the one in the book. Encourage students to do the same.

Guided Reading

- Share predictions, do some retelling using the pictures, and text-to-self and text-to-text connections during other Guided Reading lessons whether you do them with a whole-class book or with Book Club Groups.
- Research recommends the "gradual release of responsibility" to students (Pearson and Gallagher, 1983). One way to do this is to encourage students to make text-to-self connections when reading in a whole class lesson, then in small groups, and finally independently.

Working with Words

- Do a Making Words lesson with the word, **Wednesday**.

  Letters: a, e, e, d, d, n, s, w, y
  Make: as sad dad end/Ned new news weed need deed seed send ended Wednesday
  Sort: related words—end/ended, new/news; spelling patterns—-ad, -eed
  Transfer: glad, Chad, speed, tweed

- Do a Making Words lesson with the word, **surprise**.

  Letters: e, i, u, p, r, r, s, s
  Make: is us sip rip use/Sue sure pure ripe rise rises super/purse purses surprise
  Sort: related words—rise/rises, purse/purses; spelling patterns—-ip, -ure
  Transfer: clip, clips, slip, slips

Social Studies Topic: Biographies

Biographies are interesting to almost all children. The children who like information books enjoy them because they "really happened." The children who like stories like to read biographies because they are stories—true stories of other people's lives. Biographies make history come alive and thus are natural social studies links. For this Book Club Group, you will choose four biographies by David Adler. All of the biographies listed here are appropriate for children from late second grade and third grade. (Fourth- and fifth-grade teachers could use them, too.) When children write biographies in elementary school, they look more like these picture biographies than the biographies adults read and write.

Suggested David A. Adler Biographies for Book Club Groups (choose four):
- *A Picture Book of Abraham Lincoln* (Holiday House, 1989) GRL: M; RL: 3.2
- *A Picture Book of Amelia Earhart* (Holiday House, 1998) GRL: M; RL: 5.1
- *A Picture Book of Benjamin Franklin* (Holiday House, 1990) GRL: O; RL: 3.1
- *A Picture Book of Christopher Columbus* (Holiday House, 1991) GRL: P; RL: 4.2
- *A Picture Book of Dwight David Eisenhower* (Holiday House, 1992) GRL: M; RL: 3.8
- *A Picture Book of Eleanor Roosevelt* (Holiday House, 1991) GRL: M; RL: 5.2
- *A Picture Book of Florence Nightingale* (Holiday House, 1992) GRL: P; RL: 4.9
- *A Picture Book of Frederick Douglas★* (Holiday House, 1993) GRL: M; RL: 5.1
- *A Picture Book of George Washington* (Holiday House, 1989) GRL: O; RL: 3.3
- *A Picture Book of George Washington Carver★* (Holiday House, 1999) GRL: N; RL: 4.9
- *A Picture Book of Harriet Beecher Stowe★* (Holiday House, 2003) GRL: M; RL: 3.9
- *A Picture Book of Harriet Tubman★* (Holiday House, 1992) GRL: S; RL: 4.7
- *A Picture Book of Jackie Robinson★* (Holiday House, 1994) GRL: M; RL: 4.9
- *A Picture Book of Lewis and Clark* (Holiday House, 2003) GRL: M; RL: 4.9
- *A Picture Book of Martin Luther King, Jr.★* (Holiday House, 1989) GRL: S; RL: 3.5
- *A Picture Book of Robert E. Lee* (Holiday House, 1994) GRL: P; RL: 5.1
- *A Picture Book of Rosa Parks★* (Holiday House, 1993) GRL: M; RL: 5.1
- *A Picture Book of Sacagawea* (Holiday House, 2000) GRL: P; RL: 4.6
- *A Picture Book of Sojourner Truth★* (Holiday House, 1994) GRL: O; RL: 4.3
- *A Picture Book of Thomas Jefferson* (Holiday House, 1990) GRL: P; RL: 3.2

★ These books could be used for Book Club Groups during February when many classrooms in the United States talk about black history.

[Biographies]

Each book has approximately 25 pages and ends with a page of important dates and events (like a time line). The easiest biographies are the books about familiar people with only a few lines of text on the pages. An example is *A Picture Book of Abraham Lincoln*. This book follows the life of the popular United States president from his childhood on the frontier to his assassination after the Civil War. Most pages have two to four lines of text and illustrations. Some pages have only illustrations. Most children in the United States who have been in school for a year or more know something about Abraham Lincoln. Children's prior knowledge about Lincoln combined with shorter text and more illustrations makes this biography easier than the others.

A little harder than the biography about Abraham Lincoln are the two biographies, *A Picture Book of Martin Luther King, Jr.* and

A Picture Book of George Washington. Each of these books has more text on the pages than the biography of Abraham Lincoln. Most children in the United States are familiar with these two people just as they are with Lincoln. It is the text that makes them harder. One of the hardest books is *A Picture Book of Rosa Parks*. The vocabulary is the most difficult of the four by far (**boycott**, **protest**, **humiliated**, **segregated**, **discrimination**, etc). There is more text on each page, and there are several pages with just text—no illustrations!

The biography Book Club Groups in these lessons plans will last for four or five days. The children will need a day to preview and make their choices on the first day, create webs and read the books across the next two days, then do a rereading and summary writing activity on the fourth day.

Biographies for Book Club Groups Using a Variety of Authors, People, and Reading Levels:
*   *George Washington: A Picture Book Biography* by James Cross Giblin (Scholastic, Inc., 1998) GRL: N; RL: 4.6
*   *A Girl Named Helen Keller* by Margo Lundell (Cartwheel, 1995) GRL: K; RL: 2.8
*   *Meet My Grandmother: She's a Supreme Court Justice* by Lisa Tucker McElroy (Millbrook Press, 2001) GRL: M; RL: 4.1
*   *A Picture Book of Abraham Lincoln* by David A. Adler (Holiday House, 1989) GRL: M; RL: 3.2

[Biographies]

Purpose

For students to preview the four books and decide what books they would like to read

Before:	Preview the four books with the class.
During:	Have students read a page or two from each of the four books.
After:	Have students select the books they want to read and write those choices on index cards.

Preparation/Materials Needed

- A list of children randomly assigned to four groups
- Student copies (five to seven) of the four books to be previewed are placed in the four corners of the room, in baskets around the room, or at tables so that students can preview them—one title per corner, basket, or table.
- Index cards/pieces of paper and pencils/pens to write Book Club Group choices

Before Reading

Gather the class and tell them that they are going to focus on biographies this week and that you have four great biographies for them to choose from. Show students the covers of the four biographies and let them tell what they know about each person. Then, read aloud the first few pages of each of the four biographies.

During Reading

Next, hand each child an index card and ask her to write her name and the numbers one, two, and three on the card. Explain that you are going to give students 20 minutes to preview the books—five minutes for each book. Place five to seven copies of each book in the four corners of the room (on four tables, in four baskets, etc.). Randomly assign children to groups; the children in group one will go to the first set of books, the children in group two will go to the second set of books, and so on. Set a timer for five minutes and tell children that when the bell rings (or the buzzer sounds), they must move to the next corner (table, basket, etc.) and the next set of books.

After Reading

When the 20 minutes are up, have children return to their seats to write down their first, second, and third choices on the index cards. These cards help you form appropriate groups. Tell students, "I would like to give everyone her first choice, but I can't promise that. Remember that all of the books will be available for everyone to read during Self-Selected Reading after we have finished with them."

Later, look at children's choices, first at the choices of struggling readers. If *A Picture Book of Abraham Lincoln* was the choice of three and *A Picture Book of Martin Luther King, Jr.* was the choice of the other three, you would give all of these children their first choices. Next, look at the choices your advanced readers made. If four of the advanced readers chose the Rosa Parks book, give them all their first choices! If there were two excellent readers and they chose Abraham Lincoln or Martin Luther King, Jr., give them their first choices, too. These readers would also make good leaders of their Book Club Groups. Other children in the class would be given their first, second, or sometimes third choices so that each group has either five or six members.

[Biographies]

Purpose

For students to begin to read the biographies and create webs for their subjects

Before:	Talk about webs.
During:	Have students begin to read their books with their Book Club Groups and create webs.
After:	Have each group share their web and the first completed spoke with the class.

Preparation/Materials Needed

- Create and post a list of the groups based on the choices students wrote on their cards; indicate group leaders by marking with asterisks or highlighting.
- Student copies (five to seven) of the chosen books

- Chart paper or a transparency and markers for each group and one for you to use to explain webs

Before Reading

Meet with the entire class to map out the next three days of reading. Tell them how each group will meet together to read half of the book today and finish the book tomorrow. Explain how you placed a paper clip at a good stopping place, approximately halfway through each text. The groups will read to the paper clips. Ask the students in each group to take turns reading pages aloud to their groups. Show a large sheet of chart paper on which you have started a web. Explain that each group will write the name of the person they will read about in the oval in the center of their copy of the web. Then, tell them about the four lines and circles that come from the center of the web. Explain that there are "spokes" coming from each of the four circles. In the circles, have students write birth/early years, family, work, and later years/death.

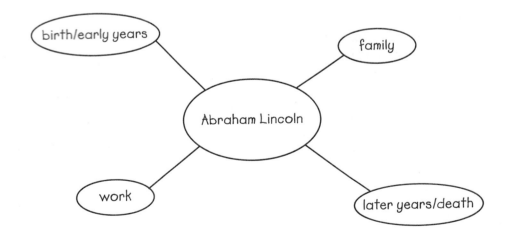

[Biographies]

Purpose

To reread their books and transfer the information from their webs into summaries

Before:	Model how to use a web to write a summary of a person's life.
During:	Have students reread their books (or parts of the books) alone or with partners.
After:	Have students turn their webs into short summaries of their subjects' lives.

Preparation/Materials Needed
- Student copies (five to seven) of the chosen books
- Completed webs from Day 3

Before Reading

Tell the class that they are all going use their webs to write paragraphs summarizing some of the important things they learned about their biography subjects. Model for them how you would use a web to write a summary.

Explain that they can reread the books by themselves or with friends, but they should write their own summaries.

During Reading

As children read, go to each child (or pair of children) and ask him to read a page aloud to you. Make notes about his fluency and word identification. As children finish their books, have them begin writing using both the books and the webs to help them.

After Reading

Combine the after-reading activity with students' writing time. Before reading, you modeled how to write a summary from a web. Use the writing time for a focused writing lesson. Give children approximately 30 minutes to write summaries of their biographies. Because they know so much about their topics and have the webs and books for support, have each child write a summary to share with the class. Each summary should contain a sentence or two about the person's birth and early life, marriage and family, what he or she is famous for, and how he or she lived in later years or died. Ask several children, one or two from each Book Club Group, to share their first drafts with the class. (If you want to post these in the classroom, students should spend some writing time revising, editing, and rewriting the summaries before you make them public.)

[Biographies]

Extensions

Self-Selected Reading

- Take time to read several biographies to the class during teacher read-alouds. Read about a variety of people, especially people and leaders that are still alive. Include some biographies of famous sports stars (for example, Michael Jordan, Tiger Woods, Venus and Serena Williams, etc.). Read both chapter books, one-day reads, and "quick reads" from reference materials and articles found on the Internet.

Writing

- Have students write reports about famous people in history. Don't just assign the reports, but show students how to read a biography or two and some reference materials, take notes, and write drafts from what they have learned.

- Encourage students to try to write their own biographies, which are called autobiographies. Use a mini-lesson to model how to do this.

Guided Reading

- Biographies are wonderful links to history. Especially helpful are the time lines and authors' notes at the end David Adler's and Jean Fritz's biographies. Making a time line of someone's life is another after-reading activity. If students are familiar with webs, then work on time lines with these biographies.

- Research recommends the "gradual release of responsibility" to students (Pearson and Gallagher, 1983). One way to do this is to teach strategies like organizing with a web for a whole-class lesson. Then, work with webs in small groups while reading. Finally, encourage students to use webs when reading independently, especially when they will be writing about the information that is being read.

Working with Words

- Do a Making Words lesson with the word, **presidents**.

  Letters: e, e, i, d, n, p, r, s, s, t
  Make: end send sent dent side pride/pried tried/tired entire resent resist desert dessert pretend present resident president
  Sort: prefixes—re-, pre-; spelling patterns—-ent, -ide
  Transfer: redo, prewriting, spent, glide

- Do a Making Words lesson with the word, **biography**.

  Letters: a, i, o, b, g, h, p, r, y
  Make: by boy pry pay pray Roy grab hair hairy gray phobia graph biography
  Sort: related words—hair/hairy; spelling patterns—-oy, -ay
  Transfer: toy, play; played, playing (related words)

[chapter 4]
Social Studies Topic:
Transportation

Wings, wheels, motors, rails, and planes fascinate many students. Forms of transportation are everywhere, and they are ready and waiting to take individuals or their packages almost anywhere in the world. The various forms of transportation available to us today make our world a much smaller place. The vehicles around us are not only interesting to young children, they are also essential to our way of life. Children ride to school on bikes and in cars, vans, taxis, and buses. They visit their families and friends in cars, buses, trains, and planes. Some children ride in trucks and on tractors almost every day. Other children take the subway or ferry to go places. Depending on where children live, they have different forms of transportation available to get them where they need to go. Many primary teachers do a transportation theme so that all children can become familiar with the various forms of transportation available today.

Suggested Transportation Books for Book Club Groups (choose four):
- *Automobiles: Traveling Machines* by Jason Cooper (Rourke Enterprises, 1991) RL: 3.9
- *Big, Big Trucks* by Melissa Bergren (School Zone Publishing, 1994) Average
- *Boats and Ships: Traveling Machines* by Jason Cooper (Rourke Enterprises, 1991) RL: 3.9
- *Cars* by Dee Ready (Bridgestone Books, 1998) RL: 1.5
- *Freight Trains* by Peter Brady (Bridgestone Books, 1996) RL: 1.5
- *Let's Fly from A to Z* by Doug Magee and Robert Newman (Cobblehill Books, 1992) Average
- *Rescue Helicopters* by Hal Rogers (Child's World, 2000) Hard
- *Terrific Trains* by Tony Mitton (Scholastic, Inc., 2000) GRL: J; RL 2.4

Whole-Class Book for Day 1:
- *Wheels, Wings, and Other Things* by Monica Hughes and Barbara Hunter (Rigby, 2000) Students are reintroduced to the many forms of transportation experienced in everyday, 21st-century life. This simple text has many of the features of informational text, including a table of contents, headings, captions, an index, and asides.

[Transportation]

Purpose

To introduce students to some nonfiction elements in a text

Before:	Introduce children to features of informational text and webs.
During:	Have children read to learn about different kinds of transportation.
After:	Let children make webs of the different modes of transportation introduced in their reading.

Preparation/Materials Needed

- Enough copies of the book *Wheels, Wings, and Other Things* for partner reading
- A web on a piece of chart paper (or a transparency) with "Types of Transportation" written in the center circle
- 8 ½" x 11" (22 cm x 28 cm) piece of paper and two to three self-stick notes for each student

Before Reading

Build anticipation for the theme by telling students, "This week, we are going to begin learning about something new. We will start our reading with this book." Hold up the book, *Wheels, Wings, and Other Things*, and ask, "What do you think we will be learning about?" Pause for a moment and then say, "Turn to a neighbor and tell him what you think we will be studying this week." After allowing a few moments of chatter say, "You're all correct. We are going to read and learn about vehicles that carry people and things. These are all types of transportation, and that is our new social studies topic."

"Today, everyone will read a copy of the book *Wheels, Wings, and Other Things* with a partner, and then create a web about transportation." Point out each of the informational text elements used on the double-page spreads (table of contents, headings, text, captions, asides, etc.). Remind students that when they read today, they have to pay attention to all of these things if they will learn everything the author wants them to know.

Finally, show students how you started your web and how you will add to the web by listing some types of transportation you read about in this book. Remove a self-stick note you have previously placed in your copy of the text and place it on the web where you will write it. Tell children that after they read, they are going to have a chance to work on webs with their partners. Hand each child two to three self-stick notes and an 8 ½" x 11" (22 cm x 28 cm) piece of paper for a web when dismissing her from the big group to begin reading.

During Reading

Have partners sit together with their desks side-by-side or at special places in the room. Have each child take a turn "whisper reading" one page at a time. Remind students that if their partners have trouble with words, they should "help" (Guess the Covered Word if you have worked with your class on that decoding strategy) or "coach" them; they should not just tell them the words. Walk around the room to check that students are using the self-stick notes to write information and mark pages to help make webs after reading. As children read and write, listen to them and make notes as needed.

[Transportation]

Be sure that when partners have finished reading, they begin to web the information.

After Reading
Give students approximately 10 minutes to work on their webs. Spend some time walking around the room and helping with this activity.

When most are finished, call the class together and share a few good webs, commenting on something you liked about each web that is shared. Post these webs where all can see or put them in a special place so that you can work with them again later if needed.

Purpose
For students to use the table of contents, index, and text to locate the informational features in this book with their partners

Before:	Introduce features of informational text.
During:	Have students reread the book and find the features in the text.
After:	Let students draw and write about something they learned in this book.

Preparation/Materials Needed
- Create and post a chart paper list with the title "Informational Text Features." (See page 190.)
- 9" x 12" (23 cm x 30 cm) drawing paper for each student

Before Reading
Have children sit with their partners with the book between them. Introduce students to the title, author, table of contents and index by asking them to find these features in the book. Show them the features in your book, and let them self-check and correct if needed. Then, look at your list of "Informational Text Features." Tell students to find these features as they read today and to be ready to share them with the whole class after reading.

[Transportation]

During Reading

Have children read the book again with their partners and find all of the items on the chart. Let partners decide how they will read today. They can take turns reading one page at a time, chorally read together, echo read one after the other, one partner can read and one partner can point to the words, or one partner can read and one partner can say something. While they read, walk around the room and listen, praising good readers and helping those who need some help. Be sure that students perform the second task—finding all of the informational text features in their books. Stop and ask each set of partners a question, such as "Where is the table of contents? Where is the index? Why did the author place that illustration there? Why is there a heading at the top of the page? How could you quickly find where _____ are written about?"

After Reading

Call the class together and use their webs from yesterday to review what they learned about transportation in this book. Then, ask all of the children to return to their seats and use the 9" x 12" (23 cm x 30 cm) paper to write sentences about what they learned about transportation. Have children illustrate their sentences, reminding them that information is often easier to understand when a person can see a picture. Suggest that they may want to include labels on their pictures. When children finish their writing and drawing, create a front and back cover, staple the papers together, and place the class book in a Self-Selected Reading basket for all of the children to read and enjoy, if they choose to do so.

[Transportation]

Purpose

To give short book talks about the four selected transportation books and allow children to preview each of the four books

Before:	Show the cover and give a book talk about each of the selections. Have students take a picture walk through the four books.
During:	Read a few pages from each book.
After:	Let students draw about something they learned from their books.

Preparation/Materials Needed

- A list of students randomly assigned to four groups
- Student copies (five to seven) of the four books to be previewed are placed in the four corners of the room, in baskets around the room, or at tables so that students can preview them—one title per corner, basket, or table.
- Index cards/pieces of paper and pencils/pens to write Book Club Group choices

Before Reading

Tell students, "Today, you will have a chance to preview the books on transportation, and then you will get to choose which books you would like to read with Book Club Groups. The books have different authors, but they are all about transportation—trains, car, planes, boats, etc. I will do a short cover talk and picture walk through each of the four books, talking about what is happening in each book." (Do this now using each of the four books you have chosen for your class to read.)

"Next, you will have a chance to preview all four of the books and choose your first, second, and third choices for your Book Club Groups. You may like one or two of the books better than the other books, or you may like them all! Your job today is to find books you want to read—ones that interest you. But, remember they must also be books you **can** read—ones where you know most of the words. So, as you look through each book today, think to yourselves, "Is this a book I **want** to read? Is this a book I **can** read?"

During Reading

Randomly assign students to four groups and choose a leader for each group. Tell students, "Today, you will move from table to table (basket to basket, corner to corner, etc.) to preview each of our Book Club Group selections. You will have five minutes to preview each book. First, look at the pictures to see what the book is about and whether it looks interesting. Next, see if you **can** read it. When the five minutes are up, I will give you a signal, and then you will move to the next table (corner, basket, etc.). (Set a timer for five minutes, or use the classroom clock and ring a bell or blink the lights.) Each group will visit all four tables reading a page or two from each book." Begin the process and after five minutes, have the groups rotate to the next set of books. Continue this process until all four books have been previewed by all of the groups.

After Reading

Display the covers of the books selected for the Book Club Groups. Have students spend a minute or two thinking about the books and

[Transportation]

which ones they liked the best. Then, have students select the three books they liked and write their first, second, and third choices on index cards. Collect students' lists and use them to create the Book Club Groups. Assign a leader to each group and create a list of Book Club Groups to post.

Purpose
For students to learn to access prior knowledge and locate and record new information

Before:	Begin a large KWL chart by filling in what students **know** (**K** column); talk about what they **want** to know (**W** column).
During:	Have each student read half of her Book Club Group selection.
After:	With students, fill in what they **learned** (**L** column).

Preparation/Materials Needed
- Student copies (five to seven) of the chosen books with paper clips marking the halfway points
- Create and post a list of the groups based on the choices students wrote on their cards; indicate group leaders by marking with asterisks or highlighting.
- A large KWL chart (page 193) as a model for the class
- A KWL chart on chart paper or a transparency and colorful markers for each Book Club Group

Before Reading
Show the students a large KWL chart and list what they know about transportation. Then, ask students if there is anything they **want to learn**. This information goes in the **W** column. (Some teachers call this the Wonder column because the response they got from their class when asked, "What do you want to learn?" was often, "Nothing!" You know your class, so decide what is best to ask.) Tell students that after they read, you hope some of their questions are answered. However, explain that often there are questions that require more research for answers. Tell students that the job today is to list their prior knowledge about the vehicles described in their books—what they already **know**—in the **K** columns of KWL charts. Remind students that proficient readers always ask questions before reading, so they should ask each other some questions and record those questions in the **W** columns. Have group members take turns

[Transportation]

reading pages. When a group finds answers to the questions, they need to be sure to have a group member record that information in the **L** column.

During Reading

Show students the posted list of Book Club Groups, tell each group where they will meet, and remind students how they will read—taking turns reading pages, beginning with the leaders. Explain that the paper clips are placed approximately halfway through the books to mark where the groups will stop reading today. Remind students that before they read, they should list their prior knowledge—what they **know** about the vehicles described in their books—in the **K** columns of KWL charts. Walk around the room and see that the Book Club Groups are also asking questions before starting to read and recording those questions in the **W** columns. Monitor each group to be sure that students are taking turns reading one page at a time and that when they find answers to their questions, they are recording that information in the **L** column.

After Reading

Call the groups together and let someone from each group share what he **knows**, and **wants** to learn, and finally what he has **learned** so far in his group's selection.

Book Club Groups [■] CD-104000 [■] © Carson-Dellosa

[Transportation]

Purpose

For students to locate and record new information and review parts of informational text features

Before:	Review the features of informational text and the groups' KWL charts.
During:	Have students finish reading their books and finding information to list on their charts.
After:	Have students finish the **L** columns of their KWL charts and make note of questions they did not find the answers to.

Preparation/Materials Needed

- Informational Text Features chart (Day 2, page 132)
- Self-stick notes for students
- KWL charts from Day 4
- Student copies (five to seven) of the selected books with paper clips marking the halfway points

Before Reading

Using the Informational Text Features chart from Day 2, review the elements of informational texts. Then, one at a time, quickly review the groups' KWL charts and talk about how students will finish their books and their KWL charts today. Remind them that when they finish reading, they should be ready to share any new information added to their KWL charts. Also, tell students that if there is any information they wanted to learn but didn't and the groups feel is important, then they should be ready to tell where they could find the answers. (Finding that information may be a homework assignment.)

During Reading

Tell students, "While reading in your Book Club Groups today, I want you to read for two purposes. First, you should be aware of the informational features of your texts as you read. You may mark them with self-stick notes." Then, have students meet with their Book Club Groups to finish reading the texts (Group members will take turns reading one page at a time.) Groups should be discussing and recording information as they read. Monitor and help groups as needed. If one group had trouble yesterday and the rest of the groups are on task, you might spend your time with that group. If so, become the "leader" and begin reading and adding any new information to that group's KWL chart.

After Reading

Call all of the groups together to share their completed KWL charts and talk about what they learned, what more they would like to know about transportation, and where they could find that information. Lead students in discussing the informational features used in their books and how these features help both reading and understanding informational books. Make sure to invite students to discuss any additional nonfiction elements they may have found while reading. If there is time after the discussion, let students write summaries about what they learned in their books today.

[Transportation]

Extensions

Self-Selected Reading

- Take time to read several picture books about transportation and vehicles to the class during teacher read-alouds. Also, include some "quick reads"—articles from newspapers, magazines, or the Internet. Encourage students to read some informational books about transportation.

Writing

- Use your mini-lesson time before students write to model some writing about transportation: a summary of a book, an interactive piece on all they have learned about modes of transportation, an informational big book about transportation written so that everyone in the class can read it, etc.
- Encourage students to try to write their own pieces about vehicles they know a lot about.
- Remind students that they can use writing time to research and write about some kinds of transportation they want to learn more about.

Guided Reading

- Reading informational books with tables of contents, pictures, charts, graphs, illustrations, captions, and indexes is different than reading fiction and requires different skills. Using content area books for Guided Reading is one way to be sure that these skills are covered. Reading about social studies topics in trade books can also give children the practice they need for content-area reading now and in the upper grades where more content-area reading is done.
- Research recommends the "gradual release of responsibility" to students (Pearson and Gallagher, 1983). One way to do this is to teach the features of informational text and KWL charts in a whole-class setting. Then, work again with informational text features and KWL charts in small groups. Finally, encourage children to use the text features and KWL charts when reading informational books that they choose.

Working with Words

- Do a Making Words lesson with the word, **transportation**.
  Letters: a, a, i, o, o, n, n, p, r, r, s, t, t, t
  Make: pot stop/spot/post/pots pint print sprint sprain strain potato potion portion station airport transport transportation
  Sort: spelling patterns—-ot, -ain; suffix—-tion
  Transfer: blot, brain, drain, vacation

- Do a Making Words lesson with the word, **airplanes**.
  Letters: a, a, e, i, l, n, p, r, s
  Make: air pair pear pail pale sail sale pain pane rain plain plane learn raise praise airplane
  Sort: homophones—pair/pear, pale/pail, sail/sale, pain/pane; spelling patterns—-air, -ail, -ain
  Transfer: chair, stair, snail, sprain

Social Studies Topic: Holidays

Some schools ask teachers not to celebrate holidays. Other schools require that teachers talk about and teach the many customs from the United States and other countries. There is a difference between celebrating a holiday and learning about it. When teachers read to students and assign certain readings about holidays, they are not celebrating the holidays but teaching about them. Students can learn even more about holidays if teachers have mock celebrations, but individual local policies may dictate what a teacher can and can't do in regards to this at school.

There are many differences in people and places in the world. Teachers do not need to celebrate a holiday to respect differences among people and places. If students are going to develop the character traits of acceptance and tolerance, they need to learn about people that are different from them and celebrations that are different from their own. This theme will help children broaden their understanding of people and their customs.

Suggested Gail Gibbons Holiday Books for Book Club Groups:
- *Christmas Is . . .* (Holiday House, 2000) GRL: K; RL: 2.6
- *Christmas Time* (Holiday House, 1982) RL: 4.1
- *Easter* (Holiday House, 1989) GRL: M; RL: 3.5
- *Halloween* (Holiday House, 1984) RL: 3.7
- *Halloween Is . . .* (Holiday House, 2002) Easy
- *Thanksgiving Day* (Holiday House, 1983) GRL: L; RL: 2.3
- *Valentine's Day* (Holiday House, 1985) GRL: J; RL: 2.7

A simple explanation of a holiday and why people do what they do is presented in each of Gail Gibbons's books. Most books have four lines and an illustration per page, but some have just two lines. These books are suitable for the end of first grade and can be read easily by both second- and third-grade classes.

Suggested Miriam Nerlove Holiday Books for Book Club Groups:
- *Christmas* (Albert Whitman, 1990) Easy
- *Easter* (Albert Whitman, 1989) Average

[Holidays]

- *Halloween* (Albert Whitman, 1989) Easy
- *Hanukkah* (Albert Whitman, 1991) Hard
- *Passover* (Albert Whitman, 1992) Hard
- *Purim* (Albert Whitman, 1992) Hard
- *Shabbat* (Albert Whitman, 1998) Hard
- *Thanksgiving* (Albert Whitman, 1990) Easy
- *Valentine's Day* (Albert Whitman, 1992) Easy

A simple explanation of a holiday and why people do what they do is presented in each Miriam Nerlove book. Most books have only two lines and an illustration on a page. These books are suitable for first- and second-grade classes.

Suggested Holiday Books by Various Authors for Book Club Groups:
- *April Fool!* by Karen Gray Ruelle (Holiday House, 2002) RL: 2.0
- *Celebrate Kwanzaa* by Diane Hoyt-Goldsmith (Holiday House, 1993) Average
- *A Family Hanukkah* by Bobbi Katz (Random House, 1993) Hard
- *Gretchen Groundhog, It's Your Day!* by Abby Levine (Albert Whitman, 1998) GRL: L; RL: 3.3
- *Hooray for Father's Day!* by Marjorie Sharmat (Holiday House, 1987) Average
- *It's Hanukkah!* by Jeanne Modesitt (Holiday House 1999) Hard
- *Mother's Day Mess* by Karen Gray Ruelle (Holiday House, 2003) RL: 2.2
- *Rhyme Time Valentine* by Nancy Poydar (Holiday House, 2003) Easy
- *Seven Spools of the Thread: A Kwanzaa Story* by Angela Shelf Medearis (Albert Whitman, 2000) GRL: N; RL: 3.1
- *This Is the Turkey* by Abby Levine (Albert Whitman, 2000) Easy

Choose a total of four books from the above lists, mixing and matching to suit the interests and reading levels of your students.

Depending on the time of year (fall, winter, spring, or summer.) your Book Club Group selections may vary. If it is the first of February, a teacher read-aloud and discussion may cover Groundhog Day. However, the December holidays might call for a variety of books covering Christmas, Hanukkah, and Kwanzaa. If Christmas is the only holiday custom in your school, then you might want to select four books on Christmas or a variety of holiday books so that your children can learn about other customs. There are so many good books on holidays that Book Club Groups are easy to do and the variety of books can help you cover the range of topics you want to cover, as well as the reading levels in your class.

Remember that background knowledge has something to do with the readability of a text. So, when reading about holidays there may be children who have not heard of some holidays, and that makes it a little harder for these children. An easy book is always about a familiar topic. These Book Club Groups will last for three days and any of the above books could be used.

[Holidays]

Purpose

For students to preview the four selected books and decide what books they would like to read

Before:	Preview the four books with the class.
During:	Have each child look at and read a page or two from each of the four books.
After:	Let children select the books they want to read and write their choices on index cards.

Preparation/Materials Needed

- A list of students randomly assigned to four groups
- Student copies (five to seven) of the four books to be previewed are placed in the four corners of the room, in baskets around the room, or at tables so that students can preview them—one title per corner, basket, or table.
- Index cards/pieces of paper and pencils/pens to write Book Club Group choices

Before Reading

Begin Guided Reading time by telling children that you have selected four wonderful books about holidays (or a certain holiday) for them to read in Book Club Groups. One at a time, show the cover of each book and using only the cover, ask students what they know about that holiday. Then, get children to predict what each book might be about. Next, tell children that they only have two days to spend on these books and they don't have enough time or copies of the books for each child to read all four books. Explain that each Book Club Group will read one book and

then hear about the other three books. Let them know that today, their job is to look at all four books and decide which books they would like to read to learn more about the holidays.

During Reading

Next, hand each child an index card and ask him to write his name and the numbers one, two, and three on the card. Explain that you are going to give students 20 minutes to preview the books—five minutes for each book. Place all of the copies of each set of books in the four corners of the room, on four tables, in four baskets, etc. Randomly assign children to groups. Have the children in group one go to the first set of books, the children in group two go to the second set of books, etc. Set a timer for five minutes and tell children that when the bell rings (or buzzer sounds), they must move to the next corner and the next group of books.

After Reading

When the 20 minutes are up, have children return to their seats and write down their first, second, and third choices. When they have trouble deciding between their first and second choices, tell students not to worry too much about the order of choices because you can't guarantee they will get their first choices or even their second choices. Tell students, "I want the groups to be about the same size, and I need to put groups together that will work well together. I promise I will give you one of your choices, and I will try to give you your first choices, but I can't promise that. But, remember all of the books will be available for everyone to read during Self-Selected Reading after we finish with them." (If you have children whose parents prefer they read or not read certain books, keep this in mind as you assign the Book Club Groups.)

[Holidays]

Purpose

For students to review or learn why people celebrate certain holidays and customs

Before:	Talk about the books, how the groups will read, and what they will do after reading.
During:	Have students read half of their books and begin lists of information they learned.
After:	Have each group share the list of information learned with the whole class. Then, compare and contrast the four books.

Preparation/Materials Needed

- Create and post a list of the groups based on the choices students wrote on their cards; indicate group leaders by marking with asterisks or highlighting.
- Student copies (five to seven) of the chosen books with paper clips marking the halfway points
- Chart paper and markers (or transparencies and pens) to begin the lists of information students learned

Before Reading

With the class gathered around you, show the cover of a holiday book that is not one of the Book Club Group selections. It could be one you read during your teacher read-aloud that day. Talk about the title and author of your book, pointing to them on the cover. Next,

open the book, read two or three pages, and model how to jot down important information about the holiday when you find it in the book. Finally, let students know the format for reading, "Today, in your Book Club Groups you will each read a page out loud starting with the leader. Then, the leader will be responsible for writing the important information on the chart (or transparency)." Let students know that they will stop approximately halfway through their books by reading to the pages you have marked with paper clips. Tell children that after their groups finish reading, they should check their lists and see if they have listed all of the important information in the first halves of their books.

During Reading

Send children to read at their groups' special places in the room. Be sure that the leaders have started reading and all of the important information is being listed on their charts, starting with titles and authors from the covers. As the Book Club Groups read, talk, and write, walk around the room and monitor, helping where needed.

After Reading

Gather the groups around you and let each share the title, author, and what they have learned so far by reading the group's holiday book. When all four groups have finished, discuss what is the same in the four books (Authors? Holidays? Other information?) and what is different (Authors? Holidays? Other information?). You might want to use a comparison chart like the example on page 143.

[Holidays]

Book	Author	Month	Religious Symbols
Christmas Time	Gail Gibbons	December	Christian
It's Hanukkah!	Jeanne Modesitt	December	Jewish
Celebrate Kwanzaa	Diane Hoyt-Goldsmith	December	none
Christmas Is . . .	Gail Gibbons	December	Christian

Purpose

For students to finish their books and their lists of information, and to "act out" two customs they read about

Before:	Review what the groups have learned and have students prepare to "act out" two customs they read about.
During:	Have students finish reading their books and making lists of information learned, as well as decide which customs to "act out."
After:	Have each group share their list, then "act out" two customs for the other groups to guess.

Preparation/Materials Needed

• Student copies (five to seven) of the chosen books with paper clips marking the halfway points
• Lists of information students learned from Day 2
• Comparison chart from Day 2

Before Reading

Quickly review the comparison chart with students and explain how the plan today is to finish the books, to gain new information and for each group to act out (pretend to do) two of the celebrations they read about.

During Reading

Send the Book Club Groups to their assigned spots in the room and have them follow the same during-reading format as yesterday (taking turns reading one page at a time and writing new information on the group charts). Once again, monitor all four groups and help as needed. Be sure that students are taking turns reading the pages, that the leaders are recording new information, and that, when finished, they

[Holidays]

decide on which customs they want to "act out" and practice. Remind students to work quietly so that they can keep their customs "secret" until they "act them out" for the whole class. Remind groups that they will not have props, but they can improvise or pretend.

After Reading

Have each group share the new information on their chart, and then "act out" two customs that the other groups must guess. If there is time, let students draw their favorite customs from any of the Book Club Group books.

Extensions

Self-Selected Reading

- Read some holiday books for your teacher read-alouds throughout the year. You don't have to be studying holidays to share the information in the books with students who might not know why we celebrate and don't come to school on certain days.
- Encourage children to read books at Self-Selected Reading time that they did not read during Book Club Groups. Put holiday books in the Self-Selected Reading book baskets throughout the year. Be sure to include both informational (nonfiction) holiday books and stories (fiction) with holiday themes.

Writing

- Encourage students to write stories about the holidays—either informational books, stories, or personal narratives. Help students with self-to-text connections that will help them write better personal narratives.
- Do an interactive Writing mini-lesson and let students share what they know about a holiday as you write (or they write).
- During your Writing mini-lesson, write a book review (not a report but a review like those in newspapers and magazines) about a holiday story or book.

Guided Reading

- Read a story about a holiday, then create and discuss a Story Map with these headings: characters, setting, beginning, middle, end, and theme (which is the holiday or holiday spirit).
- Read a story about a holiday and discuss text-to-self connections.

[Holidays]

- Read an informational book about the same holiday and discuss what information you **knew** (K) what you **wanted to know** (W) and what you **learned** (L) from this book.
- Read a holiday book and web the information in the book, and then write a report or summary of the holiday.
- Make a craft for the holiday and have students "read to learn" by teaching them how to read and follow directions. This is another guided reading skill that needs to be taught and the holidays are the perfect time.

Art

- Let children draw their favorite holiday customs from these books after reading. Art projects for the holidays are endless—drawing, painting, making collages, making wrapping paper, etc. A holiday is a great opportunity to squeeze in extra time for art (and music!). These projects will keep your children learning and put them in a festive mood.

Working with Words

- Do a Making Words lesson with the word, **holidays**.

    Letters: a, i, o, d, h, l, s, y
    Make: as is his has had hay lay old hold sold lash dash daily daisy holidays
    Sort: spelling patterns—-ay, -ash, -old
    Transfer: tray, trash, splash, scold

- Do a Making Words lesson with the word, **Christmas**.

    Letters: a, i, c, h, m, r, s, s, t
    Make: it hit sit sat hat rat/art mart chat cart chart start Chris charts Christmas
    Sort: spelling patterns—-it, -at, -art
    Transfer: smart, dart, knit, spit

- Do a Making Words lesson with the name, **Rudolph**.

    Letters: o. u, d. h, l, p, r
    Make: do up ho hop our old hold hour drop uphold/holdup Rudolph
    Sort: spelling patterns—-op, -old, -our
    Transfer: plop, stop, told, flour

- Do a Making Words lesson with the word, **Thanksgiving**.

    Letters: a, i, i, g, g, h, k, n, n, t, s, v
    Make: in kin/ink sink sing gang thank think sting stink night knight sinking thinking Thanksgiving
    Sort: spelling patterns—-ink, -ing, -inking
    Transfer: clink, swing, fling, blinking

- Do a Making Words lesson with the word, **rabbits**.

    Letters: a, i, b, b, r, s, t
    Make: as at art/rat sat bat bar tar sir stir star stair rabbi rabbits
    Sort: spelling patterns—-at, -ar, -ir
    Transfer: chat, scat, jar, fir

[Holidays]

- Do a Making Words lesson with the word, **pumpkins**.

  Letters: i, u, k, m, n, p, p, s
  Make: us in pin ink/kin ski skip skin/sink spin pink pump spunk pumpkins
  Sort: spelling patterns—-in, -ink
  Transfer: chin, thin, rink, drink

- Do a Making Words lesson with the word, **turkeys**.

  Letters: e, u, k, r, s, t, y
  Make: us use set yet key rut ruts/rust keys true rusty turkeys
  Sort: spelling pattern—-et; plurals
  Transfer: vet, vets, pet, pets

- Do a Rounding up the Rhymes lesson with the book *This Is the Turkey* by Abby Levine (Albert Whitman, 2000). Since this book is a cumulative story, you will just do the new rhymes on each page. Here are the rhymes rounded up:

out	away	bread	greens	play	high
about	day	thread	beans	day	pie
about	lot	dear	seat	fun	away
out	hot	here	eat	done	day

Next, have children underline the spelling patterns in these rhyming words:

out	away	bread	greens	play	high
about	day	thread	beans	day	pie
about	lot	dear	seat	fun	away
out	hot	here	eat	done	day

Then, discard or cross off the rhymes that do not have the same spelling patterns.

out	away	bread	~~greens~~	play	~~high~~
about	day	thread	~~beans~~	day	~~pie~~
about	lot	~~dear~~	seat	~~fun~~	away
out	hot	~~here~~	eat	~~done~~	day

Once you have rhymes that have the same rime (spelling pattern), you can use these words to read and write some new words. Tell students, "What if you were reading and came to these words: **shout**, **clay**, **head**, and **stray**? Which rhyming words would help you read these new words?" (Place the new words under the rhyming words and have the children read down the columns.)

out	away	bread	play
about	day	thread	day
shout	clay	head	stray

Ask students, "What if you wanted to write the words **spout**, **slot**, **cheat**, and **spray**? Which rhyming words would help you write these new words?" (Have children tell you how to spell the new words, then write them under the rhyming words in the correct columns.)

about	lot	seat	away
out	hot	eat	day
spout	slot	cheat	spray

You can follow the same procedure with Abby Levine's *This Is a Pumpkin* (Albert Whitman, 1997).

Science Topic: Animals

Animals are a fascinating topic for most students. Some children have pets at home and know a lot about the care and feeding of these animals. Some children live on farms and know a lot about the care and feeding of farm animals. Others have been to farms, ranches, or zoos and know things about larger animals. Animal studies are one way for students to begin reading to learn. Young children can learn how to do research, gather information, learn from that information, and write about what they learn. Today, nonfiction books are available on all reading levels from emergent readers to difficult text; no longer do children have only encyclopedias to turn to when things interest them.

Animals are subjects that are easy to find books about. Many writers, like Gail Gibbons, have spent time researching animals that children want to know more about and have written books children can read and understand. When doing a farm unit or learning about zoo animals, Book Club Groups can be one way to help children gather information.

For this topic, the whole class will read a book about penguins, then you will use Book Club Groups to read about four different animals, and finally you will encourage children to choose animals to read about and research on their own.

Suggested Animal Books for Book Club Groups (choose four):
- *All about Alligators* by Jim Arnosky (Scholastic, Inc., 1994) GRL: M; RL: 4.5
- *All about Owls* by Jim Arnosky (Scholastic, Inc., 1999) GRL: M; RL: 5.6
- *All about Rattlesnakes* by Jim Arnosky (Scholastic, Inc., 2002) GRL: L; RL: 5.5
- *Bats* by Gail Gibbons (Holiday House, 1998) GRL: O; RL: 3.8
- *Birds* by Carolyn MacLulich (Scholastic, Inc., 1996) GRL: J
- *Chicks and Chickens* by Gail Gibbons (Holiday House, 2003) GRL: L; RL: 2.8
- *Frogs* by Carolyn MacLulich (HarperCollins, 2000) GRL: J
- *Lizards* by Carolyn MacLulich (HarperCollins, 2000) GRL: J
- *Monarch Butterfly* by Gail Gibbons (Holiday House, 1991) GRL: L; RL: 4.2

[Animals]

- *Polar Bears* by Gail Gibbons (Holiday House, 1995) GRL: O; RL: 4.0
- *Rabbits* by Gail Gibbons (Holiday House, 1999) GRL: N; RL: 3.2
- *Slinky, Scaly Snakes* by Jennifer Dussling (DK Publishing, 1998) GRL: I; RL: 2.8
- *Spiders* by Carolyn B. Otto (Scholastic, Inc., 2002) GRL: I; RL: 1.9
- *Spiders* by Gail Gibbons (Holiday House, 1993) GRL: L; RL: 2.9

You may choose books from this list, as well as animal books from your own collection that will suit the reading levels of your students.

Whole-Class Book for Days 1 and 2:

- *Penguins!* by Gail Gibbons (Scholastic, Inc. 1998) GRL: O; RL: 4.1
Gail Gibbons is a wonderful author to introduce young readers to nonfiction text. She uses many features of informational text, such as diagrams, charts, and text, and makes her books readable for early readers.

[Animals]

Purpose

To introduce students to nonfiction or informational text features

Before:	Introduce nonfiction or informational text features to the class using *Penguins!*
During:	Grade 1—Read aloud; Grades 2 and 3—Have students partner read and look for text features.
After:	Discuss how informational books are different from fiction and make a list of some facts students learned about penguins.

Preparation/Materials Needed

- *Penguins!* by Gail Gibbons
- List of Informational Text Features (page 190)
- Transparency of a page with a diagram or chart from a science textbook

Before Reading

Make a transparency of a page from a science textbook (such as a fourth grade, middle school, or high school text) to introduce students to an important feature of nonfiction or informational text. For today's lesson, use just one page with a chart or diagram and discuss how this feature makes important information clear and easier to understand than just reading it. Next, show today's class book, *Penguins!* Before reading the book, take a picture walk through approximately half of the book, noting the features of nonfiction or informational text (for example, diagrams on pages 2-3, map on page 5, etc.).

During Reading

Read *Penguins!* aloud to your students if you teach first grade or if it is early in the year in second grade. If some of your students are good readers in second or third grade and you have enough copies of the book, you can have students partner-read this book. (See that each good reader is paired with someone who may need some help.) As you read the text, mention the features of the book, as well as the information included in the maps and diagrams. If children are partner reading the book, give them self-stick notes so that they can mark the pages on which they find the informational features and then share those features in the after-reading activity.

After Reading

After reading, discuss with the class how nonfiction differs from fiction, and then make a list of the information learned from the charts, diagrams, and text in *Penguins!*

[Animals]

Purpose

For students to use information from *Penguins!* to complete an Animal Research Report form

Before:	Model how to fill out the Animal Research Report.
During:	Reread *Penguins!* the same way it was read yesterday.
After:	Complete the Animal Research Report on penguins.

Preparation/Materials Needed

- *Penguins!* by Gail Gibbons
- Animal Research Report (page 191) on chart paper or transparency

Before Reading

Review the information that was learned from reading *Penguins!* on Day 1. Discuss how the book was organized and written by the author, Gail Gibbons. Ask students, "What did she have to know to write this book? If she did not know something, what do you think she did?" Then, tell students how they will find the information about penguins needed for the Animal Research Report (a paragraph frame) and how they will fill in the form after reading.

During Reading

Reread *Penguins!* aloud to your first graders or let them partner read again if students are second- or third-graders. Take time to note any information to include in the form. If students are partner reading, give them self-stick notes to write the information and mark the places where they find it.

After Reading

Discuss the information learned from this book and fill out the Animal Research Report (paragraph frame) together if you teach first grade. For second- and third-grade classes, allow partners to share information they marked in the book with self-stick notes and to fill out the form together. Then, go over the form as a class letting children self-correct by adding, deleting, and changing information as needed.

[Animals]

Purpose

To give a short book talk about the four selected books and preview them with students

Before:	Give a book talk and share some important pages from each book.
During:	Have each student preview the four books and read a page or two from each.
After:	Have students list their first, second, and third choices on index cards.

Preparation/Materials Needed

- List of children randomly assigned to four groups
- Student copies (five to seven) of the four books to be previewed are placed in the four corners of the room, in baskets around the room, or at tables so that students can preview them—one title per corner, basket, or table.
- Index cards/pieces of paper and pencils/pens to write Book Club Group choices

Before Reading

Tell students, "Today, you will have a chance to preview four books. Then, you will get to choose which of the books you would like to read with a Book Club Group. All of the books are about animals, and all four books have different authors. (Or, Gail Gibbons is the author of the books; Carolyn MacLulich is the author, etc.) I will do a short cover talk and picture walk through each of the four books, talking about the animal and giving you a glimpse at some of the information inside.

"Next, you will have a chance to preview all four of the books and choose your first, second, and third choices. You may like one or two of the animal books better than the others, or you may like them all—like me! Your job today is to find books you want to read—ones that interest you. But, you must also try to find books you can read—ones where you know or can figure out most of the words from the pictures and diagrams. So, as you look through the books with your groups today, be thinking, 'Is this a book I want to read? Is this a book I can read?'"

During Reading

Randomly assign students to four groups and choose a leader for each group. Tell students, "Today, you will move from table to table (corner to corner, basket to basket, etc.) to preview each of our Book Club Group selections. You will have five minutes to preview each book. First, look at the pictures to see what animal the book is about and if it looks interesting. Next, see if you can read it. When the bell rings (or the buzzer sounds) you will move to another table (corner, basket, etc.). You will do this four times until you have previewed all four animal books."

After Reading

On index cards, have students write the titles of the animal books they would like to read. The titles should be written beside the numbers one, two, and three for their first, second, and third choices. Allow students time in their groups to discuss why they made their choices and to ask some questions they had about these books. Use the completed index cards to assign Book Club Groups (keeping in mind the readability of books, children's reading levels and interests, and how well students work with others.)

[Animals]

Purpose
For students to gain information about animals from nonfiction texts

Before:	Talk about how and where the groups will read the books and what they will do after reading.
During:	Have students take turns reading one page each to their Book Club Groups and start group charts of what they learned.
After:	Have groups share their lists of what they learned about their animals with the whole class.

Preparation/Materials Needed
- Student copies (five to seven) of the chosen books
- Create and post a list of the groups based on the choices students wrote on their cards; indicate group leaders by marking with asterisks or highlighting.
- Chart paper or transparencies for each group to list information learned about animals

Before Reading
Meet with the entire class to map out the next two days of reading. Discuss how each group should meet together to read their book. Starting with the leader, each member of the group will read one page. Each group will read approximately half the book each day. Make sure the leader is a good coach who can help students in the group who may need it. Tell students where they will read with their groups. Remind children to be aware of the informational text features as they read the pages, and to read the charts and diagrams to their groups, as well as the text. After reading, they should begin lists of what they learned on large pieces of chart paper. (You can have them use transparencies if that works better for you.)

During Reading
Students will work together to read half of their selected books and will begin lists of facts they learned about their animals. Your job is to walk around the room monitoring and coaching the groups, noting and praising students as they read both text and informational features in their books and begin to list the information on their charts.

After Reading
Meet back as a whole class. Have each Book Club Group report on the animal they are reading about and read the information on their chart. Post all of the charts (or save the transparencies) for the groups to use tomorrow.

[Animals]

Purpose

For students to finish reading their books and fill out Animal Research Report forms

Before:	Discuss the Animal Research Report and what to do today.
During:	Have groups continue reading their books and begin to fill out their Animal Research Report.
After:	Have each group share their Animal Research Report with the class.

Preparation/Materials

- Student copies (five to seven) of the chosen books
- Group charts from Day 4 with the lists of information learned about animals
- Animal Research Report (page 191) for each group

Before Reading

Pass out the group charts from Day 4, as well as the Animal Research Reports to the leader of each group. Remind students that the Animal Research Report is the same one you used with the whole-class book *Penguins!* Review the purpose for reading and how the groups will read to the ends of their books and write new information on their charts. Finally, answer any questions students may have about the Animal Research Report.

During Reading

Send students to their groups to continue reading their animal books and listing the things they learn. When students finish reading and writing the information learned on their charts, have them begin to complete their forms together. Then, have each student draw his group's animal using markers or crayons. The pictures should illustrate information they have learned. Monitor and coach the groups as they complete the reading, begin filling out their forms together, and draw the animals they read about.

After Reading

Give one person from each group (the leader or someone else) time to share an Animal Research Report with the class. At the end of each group report, have all of the group members share their pictures. Comment on the different things the animals are doing in the students' pictures. (Are there any diagrams of the animals? Has someone drawn a picture of the animal in its habitat?)

[Animals]

Extensions

Self-Selected Reading

- Read aloud from a variety of nonfiction animal texts. Take students to the library and show them where the nonfiction texts are found. Allow students to select appropriate animal texts to read independently during Self-Selected Reading.

Writing

- Model for students how to use the charts of things they learned to write paragraphs about the animals or summaries of the books. Remind them that informational articles are better with pictures, charts, or diagrams.
- Model for students how to web information. (See pages 125-127.)
- Work together to make a nonfiction book about animals. It could be modeled after Gail Gibbons's books or Jerry Polatta's alphabet animal series.

Guided Reading

- Research recommends the "gradual release of responsibility" to students (Pearson and Gallagher, 1983). One way to do this, now that you have worked with an Animal Research Report (paragraph frame), is to encourage students to use the form as they read other nonfiction animal texts. Students could do this in small groups, with partners, or individually, depending on how much support they need.

- Talk about other features of nonfiction text that signal importance in what should be talked about:

  Fonts and effects—examples include: bold-faced type, and italic or highlighted text

  Cue words and phrases—examples include: for example, for instance, in fact, in conclusion, but, therefore, on the other hand, etc. (These and other phrases can be listed on a chart for students to refer to.)

  Illustrations and photographs—Nonfiction trade books and magazines have plenty of these!

  Graphics—Diagrams, maps, graphs, and charts can contain a lot of important information

  Text organizers—examples include: index, table of contents, glossary, appendix, etc. Students need to become familiar with and use these tools.

  Text structures—Nonfiction text may be organized by cause and effect, problem and solution, question and answer, comparison and contrast, and description and sequence. Young students can be introduced to some of these formats to help them understand the differences in how nonfiction is organized.

[Animals]

Working with Words

- Do a Making Words lesson with the word, **animals**.

  Letters: a, a, i, l, m, n, s

  Make: an am Sam aim main mail nail sail slam slim snail/slain nasal salami animals

  Sort: beginning sound—sl; spelling patterns—-am; -ail; -ain

  Transfer: jam, trail, gain, plain

- Do a Making Words lesson with the word, **penguins**.

  Letters: e, i, u, g, n, n, p, s

  Make: us in pin pig peg pen pens spin pine spine penguins

  Sort: beginning sound—sp; spelling patterns—-in, -ine; plurals

  Transfer: twin, twine, twins, grins

Other animal words to use for Making Words lessons include: chickens, turtles, duckling, kittens, monkeys, panthers, puppies, rabbits, reindeer, tigers, zebras, etc.

These and other Making Words lessons are available in the Cunningham and Hall books *Making Words* (Good Apple, 1994), *Making More Words* (Good Apple, 1997), the *Month-by-Month Phonics* series (Carson-Dellosa, 1997, 2003) and *Making Words: Lessons for Home and School* series (Carson-Dellosa, 2002).

[chapter 4]
Science Topic: Weather

People of all ages discuss the weather; wonder what the weather will be like each day; and complain when it is too hot, too cold, too wet, or too dry. Children wonder about the weather, too. Weather can be a very interesting topic for study. When we study the weather, we help students understand what makes the weather and deal with some types of weather they might fear. This is also a good topic to satisfy some budding meteorologist curiosity.

Suggested Weather Books for Book Club Groups (choose four):
- *Blizzards!* by Lorraine Jean Hopping (Cartwheel Books, 1999) GRL: N; RL: 3.5
- *The Cloud Book* by Tomie dePaola (Holiday House, 1985) GRL: N; RL: 3.5
- *Down Comes the Rain* by James Graham Hale (HarperTrophy, 1997) GRL: N; RL: 2.5
- *Feel the Wind* by Arthur Dorros (Scott Foresman, 1990) GRL: L; RL: 3.9
- *Flash, Crash, Rumble and Roll* by Franklyn M. Branley (HarperCollins, 1999) GRL: N; RL: 2.6
- *Hurricanes!* by Lorraine Jean Hopping (Cartwheel Books, 1995) GRL: P; RL: 3.5
- *Lightning!* by Lorraine Jean Hopping (Scholastic, Inc., 1999) GRL: P; RL: 3.5
- *Twisters* by Kate Hayden (DK Publishers, 2000) GRL: I; RL: 2.3
- *Weather* by Melissa Getzoff (Troll Communications, 1996) Average
- *Weather Forecasting* by Gail Gibbons (Aladdin, 1993) RL: 3.5
- *What Makes the Weather* by Janet Palazzo (Troll Communications, 1989) Average
- *What Will the Weather Be?* by Jean Dewitt (Scott Foresman, 1993) GRL: M; RL: 3.5
- *Whatever the Weather* by Karen Wallace (DK Publishers, 1999) GRL: G; RL: 1.8

Books from this list may be chosen, as well as books from your own collection that will suit the reading levels of your students.

Whole-Class Book for Day 1:
- *Weather Words and What They Mean* by Gail Gibbons (Holiday House, 1992) GRL: R; RL: 3.2 Gail Gibbons is a wonderful author to introduce young readers to nonfiction text. Through her use of diagrams, charts, and text, Gibbons uses many features of nonfiction (informational) text to make it readable for early readers. This is a great book to kick off the study of weather. As they read the book, students will learn new vocabulary that will be important to understanding basic concepts about weather.

[Weather]

Purpose

To introduce students to nonfiction text about weather and to identify important vocabulary for the study of weather

Before:	Discuss what students will read today and the vocabulary activity.
During:	You or students (depending on grade level) read half of the book *Weather Words and What They Mean* and choose four vocabulary words.
After:	Use the Vocabulary Word Map to work with the four vocabulary words and learn more about them.

Preparation/Materials Needed

- *Weather Words and What They Mean* by Gail Gibbons (multiple copies of the book if partner reading is used)
- Chart paper divided into four squares
- One self-stick note or index card per child
- Four Vocabulary Word Maps (page 192) for the class to use with the four vocabulary words

Before Reading

Ask students, "What's for reading today?" Show them the cover and some inside pages of the text. Help students discover that this is a nonfiction text all about the weather. Tell students, "We read nonfiction text differently than we read fiction. When we read nonfiction, we are looking for information. Fiction usually tells a story. As we read this book today, we will be searching for words to help us understand more about the weather." Tell students that they will be choosing four (vocabulary) words today to learn more about weather. Tell students to think about which words they want to include as you (they) are reading. Give children self-stick notes or index cards to write the words they choose. (If you are teaching second or third grade, you will want to have students read and find words with partners.)

During Reading

If you teach first grade, read the first half of the book to students. After you stop, have students vote using their self-stick notes to select four terms from the book to use on the chart. If you teach second or third grade (and you have 12-15 copies of the book) have students partner read, taking turns reading one page at a time until they get to the stopping point approximately halfway through the book. Then, with their partners, have them choose the four weather words or terms. As the partners read, walk around the class, "drop an ear" and listen, and help if needed. When you gather the whole class together after reading, you will do the same thing—let the children use their self-stick notes and vote for four words.

After Reading

When students have selected the four weather words, write one word in each of the four squares on the large chart paper. In addition, write the words on the Vocabulary Word Maps (8 ½" x 11" or 22 cm x 28 cm), one word per sheet. Work as a class (or divide into four groups) to complete the vocabulary chart, filling in synonyms and antonyms, writing a sentence with each word, and drawing a picture of each word on the chart.

[Weather]

Purpose

To finish reading this nonfiction (informational) text and identify vocabulary important to the study of weather

Before:	Discuss the vocabulary words the children chose yesterday; explain today's tasks.
During:	You or students (depending on the format) finish reading *Weather Words and What They Mean* and look for four more vocabulary words.
After:	Discuss what students learned about weather—both words and facts.

Preparation/Materials Needed

- *Weather Words and What They Mean* by Gail Gibbons (multiple copies of the book if partner reading is used)
- Chart paper divided into four squares
- One self-stick note per child
- Four Vocabulary Word Maps (page 192) for each student to use with the four vocabulary words

Before Reading

Review the information from Day 1 and discuss the meanings of the words chosen. If you teach

first grade, let students know that you will be finishing the book today, and they should listen for four more vocabulary words they want to know more about. Give each child a self-stick note. Tell students that they will be choosing another word to learn more about today. If you teach second or third grade, explain how students will partner read and look for words together again today.

During Reading

If you teach first grade, finish reading *Weather Words and What They Mean*, beginning where you stopped on Day 1 and reading to the end. Have each child write a word she wants to learn more about on a self-stick note as you read. Then, have students vote and choose four words. (If time permits, more words can be chosen and charted.) If you teach second or third grade, have students partner read. As the partners read and choose words, walk around the classroom and monitor, helping if needed.

After Reading

Use Vocabulary Word Maps (four per student) to chart the words. Monitor and coach students as they complete the individual forms today. Have all students come to the meeting area and let four students share their Vocabulary Word Maps with the class. Display the four words charted each day for students to refer to as needed when studying weather.

[Weather]

Purpose

To give a short book talk about the four selected weather books and talk about how students will preview the four selections

Before:	Give a book talk and share some important pages from each book.
During:	Have each student review the four books and read a page or two from each book.
After:	Let children list their first, second, and third choices.

Preparation/Materials Needed

- List of children randomly assigned to four groups
- Student copies (five to seven) of the four books to be previewed are placed in the four corners of the room, in baskets around the room, or at tables so that students can preview them—one title per corner, basket, or table.
- Index cards/pieces of paper and pencils/pens to write Book Club Group choices

Before Reading

Tell students, "Today, you will have a chance to preview four books, and then you will get to choose which books you would like to read with Book Club Groups. All of the books are about weather, and all four books have different authors. I will do a short cover talk and picture walk through each of the four books, giving you a glimpse at some information inside." (Do this now using each of the four books you have chosen for Book Club Groups.)

"Next, you will have a chance to preview all four of the books and then get to select your first,

second, and third choices for Book Club Groups. You may like one or two of the weather books better than the others, or you may like them all. Your job today is to find books you want to read—ones that interest you. But, also try to find books you can read—one where you know most of the words. The questions you need to ask yourselves are: 'Is this a book I want to read? Is this a book I can read?'"

During Reading

Randomly assign students to four groups and choose a leader for each group. Tell students, "Today, you will move from table to table (corner to corner, basket to basket, etc.) to preview each of our Book Club Group selections. You will have five minutes to preview each book. First, look at the pictures to see what each weather book is about and if it looks interesting. Next, see if you can read it. When the bell rings (or the buzzer sounds) you will move to another table (corner). You will do this four times until you have visited the four tables and previewed all four weather books." As students preview the books, walk around and help anyone or any group that needs it.

After Reading

Have students write the titles of the weather books they would like to read. The titles should be written beside the numbers one, two, and three for their first, second, and third choices. Allow students time in their groups to discuss why they made their choices and to ask some questions they had about these books with other members of their groups. Use the index cards to assign Book Club Groups keeping in mind the books' readability, children's reading levels and interests, and how well students work with others.

[Weather]

Purpose

For students to gain new information about weather and begin KWL charts

Before:	Explain what students will do today during reading and begin a KWL chart.
During:	Have each group read the first half of their book about weather and find some information for the **L** column of their KWL chart.
After:	Have each group fill in some facts in the **L** column of the KWL chart, then share the chart with the class.

Preparation/Materials Needed

- Student copies (five to seven) of the chosen books with paper clips marking the halfway points
- Create and post a list of the groups based on the choices students wrote on their cards; indicate group leaders by marking with asterisks or highlighting.
- KWL charts (page 193) for each group to list information about the weather
- Colorful markers
- Vocabulary Word Maps from Days 1 and 2 (if these would be helpful for your class)

Before Reading

Meet with the entire class to map out the next two days of reading. Discuss how each group should meet and read the text together. Show students a KWL chart and ask them what they **know** about weather. Use this information to fill in the **K** part of the chart before beginning to read. Write down several facts students tell you. Have them list at least three statements of things they **wonder** or **want to learn** for the **W** column. Remind students that they should look for this information as they read to add to the **learned** or **L** column. Depending on your class, you may want to review the weather vocabulary you worked with during the whole-class book (Days 1 and 2) if that would be helpful before reading.

During Reading

Have the Book Club Groups fill in the **K** and **W** columns of their KWL charts and work together to read halfway through the selected books about weather. Then, have them begin their **L** columns on the KWL charts. Circulate around the classroom, monitoring and coaching the groups. Be sure to notice and praise students as they find and list information in the **L** columns on their forms. You may decide to work with just one group if they seem to need more help than the other three groups, or spend about five minutes with each of the four groups.

After Reading

Meet together as a whole class. Allow a spokesperson from each group to share some information the group found while reading their book about weather. Have each group read their **K**, **W**, and start of their **L** columns to the class.

[Weather]

Purpose
For students to gain information about weather from informational texts

Before:	Review quickly each group's KWL chart and tell students what they will do today.
During:	Have groups finish reading their books and complete the **L** columns of their KWL charts.
After:	Have each group share their completed KWL chart, then draw weather pictures.

Preparation/Materials
- Groups' KWL charts from Day 4 to list more information learned about weather
- Student copies (five to seven) of the chosen books with paper clips marking the halfway points
- Drawing paper and crayons/markers

Before Reading
Review the purpose for reading (to gain more information about weather from their books)

and answer any questions about the KWL charts that students may have. Be sure to tell children that if their group finishes their book and KWL chart early, they can draw pictures of interesting things they learned about weather from their book.

During Reading
Send students to groups to continue reading and finish their **L** columns. As students complete the books and KWL charts, have them use markers or crayons to illustrate things they learned in their books about weather and add to the **L** columns of their KWL charts. Monitor the Book Club Groups as they work. Coach them as they complete the books, finish their KWL charts, and begin to draw interesting things they learned about weather.

After Reading
Give a student from each group time to share some information the group learned about weather from their book. Let the spokesperson from each Book Club Group use the KWL chart and drawings. Post the KWL charts and artwork in the room for all to see and admire—perhaps on your weather bulletin board!

[Weather]

Extensions

Self-Selected Reading

- Read aloud from a variety of nonfiction (informational) books about weather. Don't forget "quick reads" from newspapers and magazines. You can also use articles from the Internet about particular types of weather—hurricanes, tornadoes, snowstorms, drought, blizzards, etc.—affecting your area or other areas of the world.
- Take students to the library and show them where the nonfiction texts are found.
- Allow students to select appropriate weather texts to read independently during Self-Selected Reading.

Writing

- Use a mini-lesson to model for students how to use a KWL chart (page 193) to write a paragraph or short informational article about the weather.
- Work together to make a nonfiction book about weather. It could be modeled after Gail Gibbons's books, or Jerry Polatta's alphabet animal series.
- Model a weather report for the newspaper or television and encourage students to do the same. Will you include a weather map or picture?

Guided Reading

- When studying a topic in science, remember that reading about that topic at Guided Reading time can help children become better readers in the content areas.

Working with Words

- Do a Making Words Lesson with the word, **weather**.

  Letters: a, e, e, h, r, t, w
  Make: at rat/art/tar tear wear water weather
  Sort: spelling patterns—-at
  Transfer: flat

- Do a Making Words Lesson with the word, **blizzards**.

  Letters: a, i, b, d, l, r, s, z, z
  Make: is lid lad bid bad sad slab drab/Brad raid braid lizard blizzards
  Sort: beginning sound—br; spelling patterns—-ad, -ab, -aid
  Transfer: glad, Chad, grab, maid

- Do a Making Words Lesson with the word, **clouds**.

  Letters: o, u, c, d, l, s
  Make: do so sod cod old cold/clod loud sold scold/colds/clods could/cloud clouds
  Sort: beginning sound—cl; spelling patterns—-od, -old, -oud; plurals
  Transfer: plod, fold, mold, told

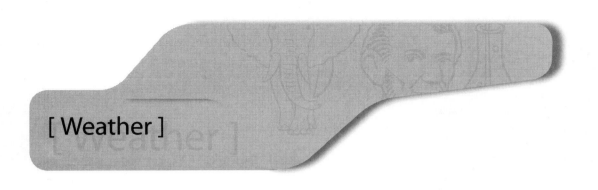

[Weather]

- Do a Making Words Lesson with the word, **thunder**.

  Letters: e, u, d, h, n, r, t

  Make: red Ted Ned/den/end hut her herd turn hunt hurt under hunted turned thunder

  Sort: beginning sound—h; spelling pattern—-ed; word ending/suffix—-ed

  Transfer: sled, sped, herded, ended

[chapter 4]
[chapter 4]

Science Topic:

Insects

Insects fascinate many children. There are at least a million different kinds of insects in the world. They are almost everywhere—on the playground, in the grass, and sometimes even in the classroom. From ants, to butterflies, to cockroaches, and more, your class is sure to enjoy studying these six-legged creatures. Get ready to learn some things along with your students!

Suggested Insect Books for Book Club Groups:
- *Bugs* by Nancy Winslow Parker and Joan Richards Wright (Scholastic, Inc., 1987) GRL: O; RL: 3.3
- *Bugs, Bugs, Bugs* by Jennifer Dussling (DK Publishing, 1998) GRL: J; RL: 2.8
- *I Can Read about Insects* by Deborah Merrians (Troll Communications, 1999) Average
- *Insects* by Robin Bernard (National Geographic Society, 1999) Hard
- *It's A Good Thing There Are Insects* by Allan Fowler (Children's Press, 1990) GRL: G; RL: 2.5
- *The World of Ants* by Melvin Berger (Newbridge, 1993) Average

Whole-Class Book for Days 1 and 2:
- *Bugs Are Insects* by Anne Rockwell (HarperCollins, 2001) GRL: K; RL; 2.5
  It's a creepy crawly creature, but is it a bug? Along with many fascinating facts about insects, children will learn how to tell what is and what isn't an insect.

[Insects]

Purpose

To find out students' prior knowledge of insects and come up with questions that motivate reading and help students comprehend informational text better

Before:	Introduce insects and see what the class knows about insects.
During:	Have students begin reading a whole-class book and look for information on insects.
After:	Model a "think aloud" and record information learned while reading today.

Preparation/Materials Needed
- A collection of books about insects (yours and borrowed books)
- KWL chart (page 193) on chart paper or transparency
- Create and post a list of partners for reading.
- Classroom set of *Bugs Are Insects* by Anne Rockwell
- Self-stick notes

Before Reading

Tell the class that you have collected some books. (Some of the books belong to you, some to the library, and some to other teachers in the school.) Then, tell students, "After looking at these books, turn to neighbors and tell them what you think we will be studying about this week." Hold up the book, *Bugs Are Insects*, and say, "You're all correct. We're going to read and learn about insects. The first two days, we will focus on this book, *Bugs Are Insects* by Anne

Rockwell. Then, we will read four different books about insects in Book Club Groups. However, before we do, I want to know what you already know about insects. We call that your prior knowledge." Point to the **K** on the KWL chart and ask, "What do you know about insects?" List what the students **know,** their background knowledge, about insects in the **K** column of the chart. If a student provides information that is questioned by other students, form the comment into a question and post it in the **W** column. The **W** column on the KWL chart is used to create questions, things students **want to know** or **wonder** about the subject.

Tell students, "By asking questions and finding answers, readers understand more about what they have read. So as you read with partners today, be sure to look for the answers to those things you wondered about." Pick up the book, *Bugs Are Insects*, commenting, "When I look at the cover of this book, a question comes to my mind, 'Are bugs the only kind of insects?' One of the reasons I'm going to read today is to find the answer. So I won't forget, I am going to write my question in the **W** column of our chart."

After writing the question in the **W** column of the chart, ask, "Do any of you have any questions you wonder about insects that can be added to this column?" Add two or three more questions. Make sure the questions include, "How do we know when an animal is an insect?" Tell students that as they read the book with their partners, they will look for the answers to these questions. "After reading, we will fill in the **L** column. That is where we put the answers to questions—what we **learned**."

[Insects]

During Reading

Pass out student copies of *Bugs Are Insects* and allow them to preview the book with their partners for a minute or two. Tell students, "Today, you are going to chorally read with your partners. That means you both read at the same time, but use your whisper voices. As you read, stop if you come to an answer to one of our questions, write the answer on one of your self-stick notes, and put it on the page where you found the answer." Tell children that they will chorally read pages 4-14 and then review the questions and any answers they found on those pages. Walk among the partners praising, encouraging, and helping them read, find answers, and jot those answers on self-stick notes.

After Reading

Gather students together in one large group with their books and self-stick notes. Using a think-aloud say, "Now that I have read these pages, I am going to reflect on what I have read and the questions we have in our **W** column. I'd like you to listen in on my thinking, so I'm going to think aloud for you." Point to your brain to indicate that you are thinking and continue, "One of our questions was, 'How do we know an animal is an insect?' I remember reading something about that. I did read it. It is right here on page 14! It says that an insect has three parts—a head, a thorax, and an abdomen. I also read that an insect has six legs. I don't want to forget what I learned, so I'm going to record these facts in the **L** column." Write, "An insect has three body parts—a head, a thorax, and an abdomen. An insect has six legs," in the **L** column of your KWL chart.

"Now, here are some more questions I have after reading that are not on the KWL chart. First, where are the abdomen and thorax on an insect? Second, are there any other animals that have six legs? I'm going to add my questions to the **W** column. Maybe I'll find the answers tomorrow. Good readers ask questions before, during, and after reading. Did any of you find any answers when reading today? Did any of you come up with more questions after reading?" Have students use the self-stick notes and books to add answers to **L** column. If children have any more questions, write them in the **W** column.

[Insects]

Purpose

For students o finish reading the text and complete the KWL chart with new information

Before:	Review the KWL chart from Day 1 and explain today's task.
During:	Have students finish reading the class book with their partners and gather new information for the KWL chart.
After:	Have students share the new information learned with the class and complete the KWL chart.

Preparation/Materials Needed

- KWL chart from Day 1
- Partner list from Day 1
- Classroom set of *Bugs Are Insects* by Anne Rockwell
- Self-stick notes

Before Reading

Use the KWL chart from Day 1 to lead a discussion that summarizes what was learned about insects.

Tell students, "Yesterday, we not only learned some interesting things about insects, we learned that good readers like you, make sure they understand the text by asking questions before, during, and after reading. These questions help good readers search for information while reading and help them understand the text better. Today, you are going to finish the book with your partners, talk about what you learned, and write some new information on self-stick notes. After reading, we will complete the **L** column on this KWL chart."

During Reading

Have the partners chorally read the rest of the book *Bugs Are Insects* in their whisper voices (as they did on Day 1). Suggest that partners stop after page 20, page 25, and the end of the book to reflect on what they read and think about the questions in the **W** column. Tell students to record any answers on self-stick notes, labeled with "A's." Tell students to record any new questions on self-stick notes labeled with "Q's." Monitor and coach the partners' reading and discussions. Take note of any interesting comments or behaviors to share with the class later.

After Reading

Gather the class together and have students place their self-stick notes in appropriate columns on the KWL chart. Share the interesting comments or behaviors you noted during observations. Let students share their responses to the questions by reading them aloud to the class. If students had questions that were not answered, come up with a list of resources for finding the answers, perhaps as a homework assignment.

[Insects]

Purpose

To give a short book talk about the four selected insect books and talk about how students will preview the four selections

Before:	Give a book talk and share some important pages from each book.
During:	Have students preview the four books and read a page or two from each book.
After:	Have children list their first, second, and third choices.

Preparation/Materials Needed

- List of children randomly assigned to four groups
- Student copies (five to seven) of the four books to be previewed are placed in the four corners of the room, in baskets around the room, or at tables so that students can preview them—one title per corner, basket, or table.
- Index cards/pieces of paper and pencils/pens to write Book Club Group choices

Before Reading

Tell students, "Today, you will have a chance to preview four books, and then you will get to choose which books you would like to read with Book Club Groups. All of the books are about insects, and all four books have different authors. I will do a short cover talk and picture walk through each of the four books, talking about the insects and giving you a glimpse at some information inside." (Do this now using each of the four books you have chosen for Book Club Groups.)

"Next, you will have a chance to preview all four of the books and choose your first, second, and third choices for Book Club Groups. You may like one or two of the insect books better than the others, or you may like them all. Your job today is to find books you want to read—ones that interest you. But also, try to find books that you can read—ones where you know most of the words."

During Reading

Randomly assign students to four groups and choose a leader for each group. Tell students, "Today, you will move from table to table (corner to corner, basket to basket, etc.) to preview each of our Book Club Group selections. You will have five minutes to preview each book. First, look at the pictures to see what the book is about and if it looks interesting. Next, see if you can read it. When the bell rings (or the buzzer sounds) you will move to another table (corner, basket, etc.). You will do this four times until you have previewed all four insect books."

After Reading

Have students write the titles of the insect books they would like to read. The titles should be written beside the numbers one, two, and three for their first, second, and third choices. Allow students time in their groups to discuss why they made their choices and to ask some questions they had about these books. Use the index cards to assign Book Club Groups, keeping in mind the books' readability, the children's reading levels and interests, and how well students work with others.

[Insects]

Purpose

For students to use KWL charts in small groups to list prior knowledge (**K**) and construct questions (**W**) that motivate reading and help comprehension

Before:	Discuss how students will use KWL charts with their Book Club Groups today.
During:	Have students read and discuss half of their books and begin their KWL charts.
After:	Have each group tell about their book and share their KWL chart.

Preparation/Materials Needed

- Create and post a list of the groups based on the choices students wrote on their cards; indicate group leaders by marking with asterisks or highlighting.
- KWL charts (page 193) on chart paper or transparency for each group to list information about insects
- Student copies (five to seven) of the chosen books with paper clips marking the halfway points
- Colorful markers
- Self-stick notes and pencils

Before Reading

Tell students, "Today, we are going to begin our Book Club Groups. Each of you will be reading a book about insects. There are some great books here. I can't wait to hear about all of the wonderful things you learned about insects when reading the four different books!" Use the KWL chart to discuss the importance of having and answering questions while reading informational books. Explain how each group will begin with the **K**, listing what they know about insects or a certain insect their book is about before they read. Then, they will come up with some questions for the **W** column. Finally, the groups will read their books, stopping every three to five pages to talk about what they learned and place "Q" and "A" self-stick notes in their books at appropriate places.

During Reading

After telling students what they will do today with their Book Club Groups and where they will meet, tell them, "When you meet in your Book Club Groups, I want you to chorally read your books, but in your whisper voices, just like with the whole-class book a couple of days ago. Make sure to stop every three to five pages to reflect on what you just read and talk about any answers you found for the **L** column. Mark the places you found the answers with self-stick notes labeled with 'A's.' Also, if you have some new questions after reading, mark the places in your books with self-stick notes labeled with 'Q's.' I will be around to help if you need me." Watch as each group lists the things they know in the **K** column and make sure they begin the **W** column with two to three questions before reading. Help any groups that need help, but the leaders (who are also good readers) should keep all of the groups on task! Monitor and coach the groups' reading and discussions. Take note of any interesting comments or behaviors to share with the class later. Make sure you praise students for their excellent reading with whisper voices, quiet discussions, good answers, and new questions after reading the text.

[Insects]

After Reading

Have students place answers and questions in the appropriate columns on their KWL charts.

Gather all of the groups together and have a representative from each group tell a little

about his group's book and share the KWL chart. Share any interesting comments or behaviors from the groups that you noted during observations.

Purpose

For students to finish the four books about insects, complete their KWL charts, and discuss interesting facts learned by each group

Before:	Review the groups' KWL charts and explain today's task.
During:	Have each group finish their book and KWL chart.
After:	Have each group share its KWL chart and any interesting facts learned.

Preparation/Materials Needed
- A list of the groups based on the choices students wrote on their cards; group leaders are indicated with asterisks or highlighting
- KWL charts from Day 4
- Student copies (five to seven) of the chosen books with paper clips marking the halfway points

- Colorful markers
- Self-stick notes and pencils
- A copy of *Bugs Are Insects*

Before Reading

Tell students, "Today, we are going to finish reading books with our Book Club Groups." Use the four KWL charts from Day 4 to discuss the books and what each group has learned so far. Explain how each group will continue to read, find answers, and possibly generate some new questions today. Review where each group will read and how (same format as Day 4—chorally reading in whisper voices). If students had problems or questions about what they were supposed to do yesterday, see that they start today with a clearer understanding of the task. If one group had more trouble than the other Book Club Groups, tell the students in that group that you will join them today.

[Insects]

During Reading

Begin this session by saying, "I know you have not completed reading your Book Club Group books. That's okay! You are all going to finish today; however, I want to talk with you about rereading text. Good readers, often reread text. When they do, they learn even more things and might have even more questions." Pick up the copy of *Bugs Are Insects* and say, "Let me show you how this happens. Last night I reread this book. When I got to page 20, I realized that I learned something new. After reading this page I learned that beetles have two pairs of wings. One pair, you can't see through. This pair hides the other pair of wings, which are clear. Now, I have a new question—which wings are used for flying? Today, your leaders will begin by rereading the text you read yesterday and asking for new questions to discuss. Then, each group will finish the book by chorally reading with your whisper voices. Next, you will discuss what you read, put your 'As' and 'Qs' in the text, finish your KWL charts, and get ready to share with the class. If your group finishes early, discuss the most interesting facts you learned." Monitor and coach the groups' reading and discussions. Take note of any interesting comments or behaviors to share with the class later.

After Reading

Have students place answers and questions in the appropriate columns on the KWL charts and begin to discuss interesting facts they learned. When most groups are finished doing this (about 25 minutes), gather the whole class together and let a representative from each group share her group's KWL chart and the facts that the group found particularly interesting. Add any fascinating comments you heard or good reading/writing behaviors you noted during observations.

[Insects]

Extensions

Self-Selected Reading

- Read aloud from a variety of insect books. Be sure to include "quick reads" from newspapers, magazines, or the Internet.
- Take students to the library and show them where the nonfiction texts are found. Allow students to select appropriate insect texts to read independently during Self-Selected Reading.

Writing

- Model for students how to use their KWL charts to write an informational article (or a paragraph) about the insect(s) they read about. Remind children that an informational article is better with a picture, chart, or diagram.
- Model for students how to web the information. (See pages 125-127.)
- Work together to make a nonfiction book about insects. It could be modeled after Gail Gibbons's books, or Jerry Polatta's *The Icky Bug Alphabet Book* (Charlesbridge Publishing, 1987).

Guided Reading

Research recommends the "gradual release of responsibility" to students (Pearson and Gallagher, 1983). One way to do this, now that you have worked with KWL charts, is to encourage students to think about what they **Know** about a subject before they read informational text and then to ask questions (**Wonder**) and search for answers (**Learn**) before, during, and after reading any informational book.

Working with Words

- Do a Making Words lesson with the word, **creature**.

  Letters: a, e, e, u, c, r, r, t
  Make: at rat cat/act ate/eat ear rear/rare tear/rate care crate/react/trace create creature
  Sort: related words—act/react; spelling patterns—-at, -ate, -ear
  Transfer: retrace, flat, smear, slate

- Do a Making Words lesson with the word, **spiders**.

  Letters: e, i, d, p, r, s, s
  Make: is sip sir rip pie dip drip ripe rise side ride pride spied spiders
  Sort: spelling patterns—-ip, -ide
  Transfer: trip, skip, slide, glide

- Do a Making Words lesson with the word, **crickets**.

  Letters: e, i, c, c, k, r, s, t
  Make: it kit sit tie irk ice rice tire/tier kite tick trick tricks crickets
  Sort: spelling patterns—-it, -ice, -ick
  Transfer: spit, slice, twice, slick

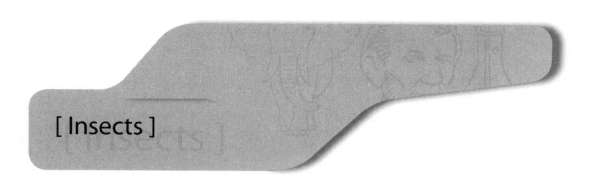

[Insects]

Art

- Draw pictures of interesting insects and label the three body parts, six legs, and other interesting features.
- Make three-dimensional insects from scrap materials and chenille craft sticks.

Science

- Mark off two squares of ground on your playground or in a park. Count how many insects are found in each square. Record the information on a graph and discuss possible reasons for differences.
- Collect pictures of insects. Organize the pictures by specific characteristics. Use resource materials to determine the insects' names.

The Science Topic: The Magic School Bus™

Joanna Cole enjoys writing science books for children, including the best-selling science series ever, *The Magic School Bus*! Ms. Cole grew up near the shores of New Jersey. She was a former teacher and children's book editor. She now writes full-time and makes her home in Connecticut with her husband and children.

Ms. Frizzle is the strangest teacher in the school and the main character in *The Magic School Bus* series. She wears strange dresses, and sometimes she wears strange shoes. She also believes in "hands-on science" and has the children grow green mold on old pieces of bread and build models of garbage dumps, as well as dinosaurs. Students in Ms. Frizzle's class go on weird field trips with her and her wonderfully wacky school bus. Whenever the class studies something, Ms. Frizzle really gets into it, eventually taking her class on an imaginary trip to learn more about that subject.

Choose any of these books to read and study to learn more about science topics or review the year with several books about topics you have studied. It is always fun to include some books you have not studied and learn more about science and science topics.

Suggested *The Magic School Bus* Books for Book Club Groups (choose four):
- *The Magic School Bus: At the Waterworks* (Scholastic, Inc., 1990) GRL: P; RL: 3.9
- *The Magic School Bus: In the Time of the Dinosaurs* (Scholastic, Inc., 1994) GRL: P; RL: 3.3
- *The Magic School Bus: Inside a Beehive* (Scholastic, Inc., 1996) GRL: P; RL: 3.7
- *The Magic School Bus: Inside the Earth* (Scholastic, Inc., 1987) GRL: P; RL: 3.6
- *The Magic School Bus: Inside the Human Body* (Scholastic, Inc., 1989) GRL: P; RL: 3.9
- *The Magic School Bus: Inside a Hurricane* (Scholastic, Inc., 1995) GRL: P; RL: 3.6
- *The Magic School Bus: Lost in the Solar System* (Scholastic, Inc., 1990) GRL: P; RL: 3.9
- *The Magic School Bus: On the Ocean Floor* (Scholastic, Inc., 1992) GRL: P; RL: 3.5

The reading levels of all of these books are approximately the same. The book on dinosaurs may be easier for many children who know a lot about dinosaurs by third grade. Any book will be easier after studying that topic because the children will have the background knowledge

[*The Magic School Bus*]

and vocabulary to read it. If you teach third grade and your class has readers who are not reading on grade level, be sure each Book Club Group has a student teacher/leader who can and will support the students who find these books difficult. Also, be sure to assign a during-reading strategy that will require all students to read the text independently each day. By working together in cooperative groups, third-grade students can find success and have fun with these books.

[*The Magic School Bus*]

Purpose

To give a short book talk about the four selected books

Before:	Give a cover talk and picture walk and share some important pages from each of the four books.
During:	Have children preview the four books and read a page or two from each book.
After:	Have children list their first, second, and third choices.

Preparation/Materials Needed

- List of children randomly assigned to four groups
- Student copies (five to seven) of the four books to be previewed are placed in the four corners of the room, in baskets around the room, or at tables so that students can preview them—one title per corner, basket, or table.
- Index cards/pieces of paper and pencils/pens to write Book Club Group choices

Before Reading

Tell students, "Today, you will have a chance to preview four books, and then you will get to choose which books you would like to read with Book Club Groups. All of the books are about Ms. Frizzle and class trips on The Magic School Bus to learn more about things in science. All four books have the same author, Joanna Cole. I will do a cover talk and picture walk through each of the four books, giving you a glimpse of the book and some information inside." (Do this now using each of the four books you have chosen for Book Club Groups.)

"Next, you will have a chance to preview all four of the books and select your first, second, and third choices for your Book Club Groups. You may like one or two of the books better than the others, or you may like them all. Your job today is to find books you want to read—ones that interest you. But, also try to find books you can read—ones where you know most of the words. The questions you need to ask yourselves are, "Is this a book I want to read? Is this a book I can read?"

During Reading

Randomly assign students to four groups and choose a leader for each group. Tell students, "Today, you will move from table to table (corner to corner, basket to basket, etc.) to preview each of our Book Club Group selections. You will have five minutes to preview each book. First, look at the pictures to see what the book is about and if it looks interesting. Next, see if you can read it. When the bell rings (or the buzzer sounds), you will move to another table (corner, basket, etc.). You will do this four times until you have previewed all four books." As students preview the books, walk around and help anyone or any group that needs a little extra help or coaching.

[*The Magic School Bus*]

After Reading

Have students write the titles of the books they would like to read. The titles should be written beside the numbers one, two, and three for their first, second, and third choices. Allow students time in their groups to discuss why they made

their choices and to ask some questions they had about these books. Use the index cards to assign Book Club Groups, keeping in mind children's interests, reading levels, and how well they work with other students.

Purpose

For students to read and talk about the narrative elements in each book

Before:	Preview a book in *The Magic School Bus* series and talk about the three kinds of text in each book.
During:	Have each group read and discuss the "story" in their book.
After:	Have each group shares the "story" in their book.

Preparation/Materials Needed

- Create and post a list of the groups based on the choices students wrote on their cards; indicate group leaders by marking with asterisks or highlighting.
- Student copies (five to seven) of the chosen books

- Beach ball for the after-reading activity
- Optional: individual Story Maps (page 185)

Before Reading

Tell the class, "Sometimes you come across a book that is primarily information but is written in story form. The books you will read today are examples of this. (Show the text as you talk about this. If you have a big book to use, that it is even better!) Really these books have three different kinds of text: fiction (a story about an imaginary field trip), a cartoon (a side story written in word balloons), and nonfiction or information (written as notes on the sides of some pages). Joanna Cole is the author of all of the books in this popular reading series. Each book contains lots of science information along with a story. Today, your group will go on an imaginary field trip to the waterworks, the ocean floor, the solar system, or inside the human body." (Use whichever subjects are featured in the books for your Book Club Groups.)

[*The Magic School Bus*]

"But, it can be very hard to figure out how to read one of these books. Some of you may have wondered as you looked at these pages, What do you read first, and how do you keep up with the story and learn new information simultaneously? As you open your books with your groups today, I want each leader to ask, 'What's for reading?' At that time, you should look through your books and see what you will read about today, but look only at the cover and pictures. After a minute, each leader will let two or three students from the group tell what they saw and what they expect to happen in this book. Then, you will take turns reading a page each out loud to the group. Just read the text to see if your predictions were right. When you finish, discuss your science stories with your groups. Then, each group will choose someone to share their story with the whole class. I will toss the beach ball and ask several children in each group to answer some of the questions." Send children to their appointed tables. As they read and discuss their "stories," circulate and help as needed.

During Reading

Have the group leaders gather their Book Club Groups around their appointed tables and ask,

"What's for reading?" Children will begin looking through their books, previewing the covers, and looking at as many pages as they can before they are asked by the leaders, "What do you think we will read about today?" From the pictures in their books, children can tell where the field trips in these books will take them and what they will see. Walk around the room, seeing that all of the groups are on task and listening to a few children in each group read. Ask each group who is going to give a brief summary of the trip and make a note of it.

After Reading

Call the whole class back together but ask group members to sit near each other. One by one, call on the groups and ask each group's spokesperson to give a summary. Then, toss the beach ball to three or four students and have each one answer a question about the narrative elements of his book. Repeat this four times so that each group gets a turn to talk about their book and show that the group members understand the narrative elements. If you want or need a grade for this reading lesson, you might hand each student a Story Map to work on individually when he returns to his seat.

[*The Magic School Bus*]

Purpose

For students to continue reading the books and talk about the text in the word balloons

Before:	Talk about cartoons, how they are written, and word balloons.
During:	Have each group read and discuss the "cartoons" or side remarks.
After:	Have each group share some of the "word balloons" and side remarks. Then, have students draw word balloons with both the pictures and text.

Preparation/Materials Needed

- Create and post a list of the groups based on the choices students wrote on their cards; indicate group leaders by marking with asterisks or highlighting.
- Cut cartoons with word balloons from the newspaper to show the class.
- Student copies (five to seven) of the chosen books
- Drawing paper, crayons, and pencils for the after-reading activity

Before Reading

Tell students, "We talked about your books having three different types of text. Yesterday, we worked on the narrative. Today, we will work on the word balloons that look like cartoons on each page. (You might want to bring in some cartoons with word balloons from the newspaper to share with your class.) The word balloons are not part of the narrative story, but they add to the book or the author would not have placed them there. Your job today is to read the word balloons. I think the easiest way is to assign students to be characters to read what they say and make a play of it! Each leader will look through the text, find who speaks, and assign those parts. I will give each group a large piece of paper to write who is assigned to what part. Post it so that you won't forget. When each group finishes reading, talk about and decide on your favorite word balloons, and then be ready to draw them, just like Joanna Cole did in her books."

During Reading

Send the groups to their tables. As parts are assigned and the children read, walk around the room and see if all children are on task and if any groups or leaders need help. After about 20-25 minutes, signal the end of reading.

After Reading

Call the groups together and let each group share some favorite things they read in the word balloons in their book. Be sure you have children tell you why they think the author put the balloons in the book. When each group has shared, have children go back to their desks and draw their favorite word balloons from their books. Their word balloons need to be complete with both the drawings and the text inside the balloons.

[*The Magic School Bus*]

Purpose

For students to continue reading the books and talk about the information in the notes on the sides of the pages

Before:	Talk about the "information" given as notes in each book.
During:	Have each group read and discuss the "information."
After:	Have each group share some important "information" noted in their book.

Preparation/Materials Needed

- A list of the groups based on the choices students wrote on their cards, with group leaders indicated with asterisks or highlighting
- Student copies (five to seven) of the chosen books
- Notebook paper and pencils (or a transparency and markers) for each group

Before Reading

Tell students, "We talked about your books having three different types of text. We have worked on the narrative text and the word balloons. Today, we will work on the information written like notes on notebook paper. Many pages in *The Magic School Bus* books have these notes, but not all of them do. Your job today is to find and read all of the notes and to gather the information that is important to your groups' science topics. I think the easiest way to do this is to assign one person to read the notes and another to make a list after you discuss what to write as a group. Don't copy every note word for word, but decide how you can summarize or condense the information to report it to the class. I will give each group a piece of paper and a pencil (or a transparency and a pen) for the person who will take notes. When you finish, you will share these lists with the whole class."

During Reading

Send the groups to their tables. Have each group leader select a reader and a different person to be the writer. (Some leaders will select themselves for one of these roles!) Have the groups begin reading, discussing, and writing lists of facts from their books. After about 20-25 minutes, signal the end of reading.

After Reading

Call the groups together and let each group share their list of things the group members learned by reading the notes in their book. Be sure you have children tell you why they think the author put the information in the book that way. When each group has shared, have children go back to their desks and do a "quick write," listing something new they learned from each book—four things in all.

[*The Magic School Bus*]

Purpose

For students to compare and contrast four books in this science series, discussing what is alike and what is different

Before:	Compare the four books and talk about how are they alike and different.
During:	Have children reread their books any way they wish.
After:	Have each child partner with a child from a different group and let the partners share their favorite parts from their books. Or, have each child draw or write about his favorite part when he finishes reading.

Preparation/Materials Needed

- A list of the groups based on the choices students wrote on their cards, with group leaders indicated with asterisks or highlighting
- Student copies (five to seven) of the chosen books
- A transparency divided in half with a line; one side labeled "Alike" and the other side labeled "Different"

Before Reading

With the whole class, talk about what was alike in the books (Ms. Frizzle, her crazy clothes, field trips, the "magic" school bus, the children, science topics, etc.) and write those things on the "Alike" side of the transparency. Then, talk about the differences (where they went, what happened, what they learned, etc.) and write those things on the "Different" side of the transparency. Explain to children that they will read their books silently by themselves, any way they wish (page by page, one type of text at a time, or a combination), at their desks today.

During Reading

Have children get their books and go back to their seats to read silently and alone. Having read the text three times, students should be able to decide if they can read every page—page by page—or read the three different text types by themselves one at a time again. For some children, one way is better than the other, so you need to circulate, stop by several children, and ask them to read out loud for you. Help children who need assistance. If you have two or three students who would do better in a small, pull group with you, then do this.

After Reading

Let each child partner with someone nearby who has read a different book. Have the partners share their favorite parts. Or, you could have each child write a sentence or draw a picture of her favorite part when she finishes reading.

[*The Magic School Bus*]

Extensions

Self-Selected Reading
- Read aloud some of the other books in *The Magic School Bus* series.
- During Self-Selected Reading time, encourage students to read books from *The Magic School Bus* series that they did not read for Book Club Groups.

Writing
- Model for students how to write cartoons.
- Model for students how to take notes on a field trip (as the characters did in each of the books) and assign note taking as part of your next field trip.
- Have students write reports or summaries of the next field trip—all facts, no fiction!

Guided Reading
- Research recommends the "gradual release of responsibility" to students (Pearson and Gallagher, 1983). One of the best ways to ensure that all students can read assigned text is to take them through texts that are different or "new" to your class or most readers in the class. Then, work with similar text in small groups—use Book Club Groups! Finally, encourage children to choose this type of text when reading books during Self-Selected Reading.

Working with Words
- Do a Making Words lesson with the word, **adventures**.

  Letters: a, e, e, u, d, n, r, s, t, v
  Make: at rat sat ear near dear deer nest rest vest tune tuner enter tender nature venture adventures
  Sort: spelling patterns—-at, -ear, -est; homophones—dear/deer
  Transfer: scat, fear, smear, pest

- Do a Making Words lesson with the word, **hurricanes**.

  Letters: a, e, i, u, c, h, n, r, r, s
  Make: as air hair hare care/race cash racer ranch chair share scare search rancher cashier hurricanes
  Sort: spelling patterns—-air, -are; suffix—-er
  Transfer: pair (noun, meaning two), stair, dare, searcher

- Do a Making Words lesson with the word, **imagination**.

  Letters: a, a, e, i, i, i, o, g, m, n, n, t
  Make: in an ago tan main gain again among giant nation maintain imagination
  Sort: spelling patterns—-ain, -an; suffix—-tion; prefix—a-
  Transfer: vacation, ahead, plan, plain

Appendix

Reproducibles

References

Arthur's Glasses

Materials Needed:

- 4 brown chenille craft sticks
- Lots of patience as you go through the directions step-by-step

1. Create a loop in two of the chenille craft sticks by bending and twisting them until they look like two balloons.

2. Cut about one inch of each of the two ends of the looped chenille craft sticks.

3. Wind these two shortened ends together. This is the "frame" piece of your glasses.

4. Take the two unused chenille craft sticks and cut off approximately one fourth of the length.

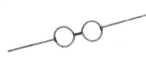

5. Take these two shortened pieces and wind one end around each side of the "frame" piece to create ear pieces.

6. Bend the ear pieces back at right angles.

7. Finally, put on the glasses and curl the ends around your ears to create a custom fit.

(Activity created by Regan McKay.)

From *Guided Reading the Four-Blocks® Way* by Cunningham, Hall, and Cunningham (Carson-Dellosa, 2000)

Story Map

Name _____ Date _____

Title: _____

Author: _____

Who are the main characters?

_____

_____

_____

What is the setting?

_____

_____

_____

What happens in the story?

Beginning: _____

_____

Middle: _____

_____

End: _____

_____

Problem and Solution Chart

Name _____ Date _____

Title: _____

Author: _____

Who are the main characters?

_____

_____

_____

What is the problem?

_____

_____

_____

What are the 3 possible solutions for the problem?

1. _____

2. _____

3. _____

What is the solution from the story?

_____

_____

_____

Preview and Predict Form

Name _____ Date _____

Title: _____

Author: _____

I predict . . .

_____

Title: _____

Author: _____

I predict . . .

_____

Title: _____

Author: _____

I predict . . .

_____

Title:
_____

Author:
_____

I predict . . .

_____

My choices: 1. _____

2. _____

3. _____

Text-to-Self Connections

Name _____ Date _____

When I read . . .	. . . it reminds me of . . .

Questioning Web

Name _____ Date _____

Title: _____

Write questions about the text in the middle of the circle below. Write thoughts about the text on the lines connected to the circle. Write a summary of your thoughts about the text on the lines below the Questioning Web.

_____

_____

_____

_____

_____

Informational Text Features

- Title

- Author

- Table of Contents

- Headings

- Text

- Illustrations

- Captions

- Index

Animal Research Report

Name _____ Date _____

Title: _____

Author: _____

Illustrator: _____

Report:

One thing I already knew about _____

was _____

_____.

From the book, I learned that _____

_____.

Some interesting facts are: _____,

_____ , and _____

_____.

The most interesting thing I learned was _____

_____.

Draw a picture of your animal on the back of this page.

Vocabulary Word Map

Name _____ Date _____

Write an antonym:_____

Vocabulary Word

Use it in a sentence: _____

_____.

Draw a picture or relate the word to yourself.

Adapted from Word Map (v.2) by Raymond C. Jones (*www.readingquest.org*).

KWL Chart

Name _____ Date _____

K What I Already **Know**	W What I **Wonder** or **Want to Know**	L What I **Learned**

[Professional References]

Cunningham, P. M. (2004). *Making Names: Hands-On Spelling and Phonics Lessons.* Greensboro, NC: Carson-Dellosa.

Cunningham, P. M. and Allington, R. L. (2003). *Classrooms That Work: They Can ALL Read and Write.* Boston, MA: Allyn and Bacon.

Cunningham, P. M. and Hall, D. P. (1994). *Making Words: Multilevel, Hands-On, Developmentally Appropriate Spelling and Phonics Activities.* Carthage, IL: Good Apple.

Cunningham, P. M. and Hall, D. P. (1997). *Making More Words: Multilevel, Hands-On Phonics and Spelling Activities.* Carthage, IL: Good Apple.

Cunningham, P. M. and Hall, D. P. (1997, 2003). *Month-by-Month Phonics for First Grade.* Greensboro, NC: Carson-Dellosa.

Cunningham, P. M. and Hall, D. P. (1997, 2003). *Month-by-Month Phonics for Second Grade.* Greensboro, NC: Carson-Dellosa.

Cunningham, P. M. and Hall, D. P. (1997, 2003). *Month-by-Month Phonics for Third Grade.* Greensboro, NC: Carson-Dellosa.

Cunningham, P. M., Hall, D. P., and Cunningham, J. M. (2000). *Guided Reading the Four-Blocks® Way.* Greensboro, NC: Carson-Dellosa.

Duke, N. V. and Bennett-Armistead, V. S. (2004). *Reading and Writing Informational Text in the Primary Grades: Research-Based Practices.* New York, NY: Scholastic, Inc.

Harris, T. L. and Hodges, R. E. (eds.) (1995). *The Literacy Dictionary.* Newark, DE: International Reading Association.

Harvey, S. and Goudvis, A. (2000). *Strategies That Work: Teaching Comprehension to Enhance Understanding.* York, ME: Stenhouse.

Keene, E. O. and Zimmermann, S. (1997). *Mosaic of Thought: Teaching Comprehension in a Reader's Workshop.* Portsmouth, NH: Heinemann.

Miller, D. (2002). *Reading with Meaning: Teaching Comprehension in the Primary Grades.* York, ME: Stenhouse.

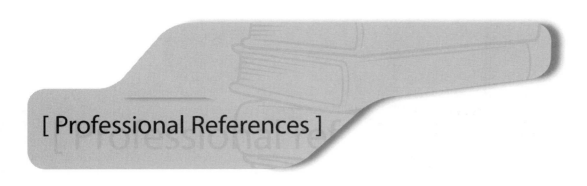

[Professional References]

Pearson, P. D., and Gallagher, M. (1983). "The Instruction of Reading Comprehension." *Contemporary Educational Psychology, 8* (3), 317-344.

Tierney, R. and Cunningham, J. (1983). "Research on Teaching Reading Comprehension." In P. D. Pearson (Ed.) *Handbook of Reading Research*. New York, NY: Longman, pp. 609-655.

[Children's Books Cited]

26 Fairmont Avenue Series by Tomie DePaola (Putnam Publishing Group)

Alexander and the Terrible, Horrible, No Good, Very Bad Day by Judith Viorst (Aladdin Books, 1972)

All about Alligators by Jim Arnosky (Scholastic, Inc., 1994)

All about Owls by Jim Arnosky (Scholastic, Inc., 1999)

All about Rattlesnakes by Jim Arnosky (Scholastic, Inc., 2002)

All I See by Cynthia Rylant (Orchard Books, 1988)

Amelia Bedelia by Peggy Parish (HarperTrophy, 1992)

Amelia Bedelia and the Baby by Peggy Parish (Avon, 1996)

Amelia Bedelia and the Surprise Shower by Peggy Parish (HarperTrophy, 1995)

Amelia Bedelia Goes Camping by Peggy Parish (HarperTrophy, 2003)

Amelia Bedelia Helps Out by Peggy Parish (Avon, 1997)

Amelia Bedelia's Family Album by Peggy Parish (HarperTrophy, 2003)

Appelemando's Dreams by Patricia Polacco (The Putnam & Grosset Group, 1997)

April Fool! by Karen Gray Ruelle (Holiday House, 2002)

The Art Lesson by Tomie dePaola (G. P. Putnam's Sons, 1989)

Arthur Writes a Story by Marc Brown (Little, Brown and Co., 1996)

Arthur's Computer Disaster by Marc Brown (Little, Brown and Co., 1997)

Arthur's Pet Business by Marc Brown (Little, Brown and Co., 1997)

Arthur's Nose by Marc Brown (Little, Brown and Co., 1979)

[Children's Books Cited]

Arthur's Teacher Trouble by Marc Brown (Little, Brown and Co., 1986)

Arthur's Thanksgiving by Marc Brown (Scholastic, Inc., 1983)

Arthur's Tooth by Marc Brown (Little, Brown and Co., 1985)

Automobiles: Traveling Machines by Jason Cooper (Rourke Enterprises, 1991)

Babushka's Doll by Patricia Polacco (Aladdin Books, 1990)

The Baby Sister by Tomie dePaola (Penguin Putnam Books, 1996)

Bats by Gail Gibbons (Holiday House, 1998)

Big Anthony: His Story by Tomie dePaola (Puffin Books, 1998)

Big, Big Trucks by Melissa Bergren (School Zone Publishing, 1994)

Birds by Carolyn MacLulich (Scholastic, Inc., 1996)

Birthday Presents by Cynthia Rylant (Orchard Books, 1991)

Blizzards! by Lorraine Jean Hopping (Cartwheel Books, 1999)

Boats and Ships: Traveling Machines by Jason Cooper (Rourke Enterprises, 1991)

Bugs by Nancy Winslow Parker and Joan Richards Wright (Scholastic, Inc. 1987)

Bugs Are Insects by Anne Rockwell (HarperCollins, 2001)

Bugs, Bugs, Bugs by Jennifer Dussling (DK Publishing, 1998)

The Butterfly Book by Gail Gibbons (HarperTrophy, 1990)

Cars by Dee Ready (Bridgestone Books, 1998)

The Cat in the Hat by Dr. Seuss (Random House, 1985)

[Children's Books Cited]

Celebrate Kwanzaa by Diane Hoyt-Goldsmith (Holiday House, 1993)

Charlie Needs a Cloak by Tomie dePaola (Simon and Schuster, 1982)

Chester's Way by Kevin Henkes (Greenwillow Books, 1998)

The Chicken Sisters by Laura Numeroff (HarperTrophy, 1999)

Chicken Sunday by Patricia Polacco (The Putnam & Grosset Group, 1992)

Chicks and Chickens by Gail Gibbons (Holiday House, 2003)

Chimp's Don't Wear Glasses by Laura Numeroff (Scholastic School Market, 1995)

Christmas by Miriam Nerlove (Albert Whitman, 1990)

Christmas Is . . . by Gail Gibbons (Holiday House, 2000)

Christmas Time by Gail Gibbons (Holiday House, 1982)

Chrysanthemum by Kevin Henkes (Greenwillow Books, 1991)

Click, Clack, Moo: Cows That Type by Doreen Cronin (Simon and Schuster, 2000)

The Cloud Book by Tomie dePaola (Holiday House, 1985)

Come Back, Amelia Bedelia by Peggy Parish (HarperTrophy, 1995)

Dandelions by Eve Bunting (Voyager, 1995)

Days with Frog and Toad by Arnold Lobel (HarperTrophy, 1984)

A Day's Work by Eve Bunting (Clarion Books, 1994)

Dogs Don't Wear Sneakers by Laura Numeroff and Felicia Bond (Aladdin Paperbacks, 1996)

Down Comes the Rain by James Graham Hale (HarperTrophy, 1997)

[Children's Books Cited]

Easter by Gail Gibbons (Holiday House, 1989)

Easter by Miriam Nerlove (Albert Whitman, 1989)

A Family Hanukkah by Bobbi Katz (Random House, 1993)

Families by Ann Morris (Steck-Vaughn, 2001)

Feel the Wind by Arthur Dorros (Scott Foresman, 1990)

Fireflies by Julie Brinkloe (Scott Foresman, 1986)

Flash, Crash, Rumble and Roll by Franklyn M. Branley (HarperCollins, 1999)

Fly Away Home by Eve Bunting (Clarion Books, 1991)

The Foot Book by Dr. Seuss (Random House, 1988)

Freight Trains by Peter Brady (Bridgestone Books, 1996)

Frog and Toad All Year by Arnold Lobel (HarperTrophy, 1984)

Frog and Toad Are Friends by Arnold Lobel (HarperTrophy, 1979)

Frog and Toad Together by Arnold Lobel (HarperTrophy, 1979)

Frogs by Carolyn MacLulich (HarperCollins, 2000)

George Washington: A Picture Book Biography by James Cross Giblin (Scholastic, Inc., 1998)

A Girl Named Helen Keller by Margo Lundell (Cartwheel, 1995)

Going Home by Eve Bunting (HarperTrophy, 1996)

Good Work, Amelia Bedelia by Peggy Parrish (HarperTrophy, 2003)

Grandpa's Face by Eloise Greenfield (The Putnam & Grosset Group, 1996)

[Children's Books Cited]

Grasshopper on the Road by Arnold Lobel (HarperTrophy, 1986)

Green Eggs and Ham by Dr. Seuss (Random House, 1988)

Gretchen Groundhog, It's Your Day! by Abby Levine (Albert Whitman, 1998)

Halloween by Gail Gibbons (Holiday House, 1984)

Halloween by Miriam Nerlove (Albert Whitman, 1989)

Halloween Is . . . by Gail Gibbons (Holiday House, 2002)

Hanukkah by Miriam Nerlove (Albert Whitman, 1991)

Henry and Mudge and the Forever Sea by Cynthia Rylant (Aladdin Paperbacks, 1993)

Henry and Mudge and the Long Weekend by Cynthia Rylant (Aladdin Paperbacks, 1996)

Henry and Mudge and the Sneaky Crackers by Cynthia Rylant (Aladdin Paperbacks, 1999)

Henry and Mudge and the Snowman Plan by Cynthia Rylant (Aladdin Paperbacks, 2000)

Henry and Mudge in the Family Trees by Cynthia Rylant (Aladdin Paperbacks, 1998)

Henry and Mudge: The First Book by Cynthia Rylant (Aladdin Paperback, 1990)

Henry and Mudge under the Yellow Moon by Cynthia Rylant (Aladdin Paperbacks, 2001)

Hooray for Father's Day! by Marjorie Sharmat (Holiday House, 1987)

Hop on Pop by Dr. Seuss (Random House, 1963)

How Many Days to America? by Eve Bunting (Clarion Books, 1990)

Hurricanes! by Lorraine Jean Hopping (Cartwheel Books, 1995)

I Can Read About Insects by Deborah Merrians (Troll Communications, 1999)

[Children's Books Cited]

I Can Read with My Eyes Shut! by Dr. Seuss (Random House, 1978)

The Icky Bug Alphabet Book by Jerry Pallotta (Charlesbridge Publishing, 1987)

If You Give a Moose a Muffin by Laura Numeroff (HarperCollins, 1991)

If You Give a Mouse a Cookie by Laura Numeroff (HarperCollins, 1985)

If You Give a Pig a Pancake by Laura Numeroff (HarperCollins, 1998)

If You Take a Mouse to School by Laura Numeroff (HarperCollins, 2002)

Insects by Robin Bernard (National Geographic Society, 1999)

Ira Sleeps Over by Bernard Waber (Scott Foresman, 1975)

It's A Good Thing There Are Insects by Allan Fowler (Children's Press, 1990)

It's Hannukkah! by Jeanne Modesitt (Holiday House 1999)

Jamie O'Rourke and the Big Potato: An Irish Folktale by Tomie dePaola (Penguin Putnam Books for Young Readers, 1992)

Jessica by Kevin Henkes (Greenwillow Books, 1989)

Julius: The Baby of the World by Kevin Henkes (Greenwillow Books, 1990)

Jumanji by Chris Van Allsburg (Houghton Mifflin, 1980)

Just Grandma and Me by Mercer Mayer (Golden Books, 1985)

Just Grandpa and Me by Mercer Mayer (Golden Books, 2001)

Just Me and My Mom by Mercer Mayer (Goldencraft, 1990)

Just Plain Fancy by Patricia Polacco (Dragonfly Books, 1990)

The Keeping Quilt by Patricia Polacco (Aladdin Paperbacks, 1988)

[Children's Books Cited]

The Knight and the Dragon by Tomie dePaola (Putnam, 1980)

Laura Numeroff's 10-Step Guide to Living with Your Monster by Laura Numeroff (Laura Geringer, 2002)

The Legend of the Bluebonnet by Tomie dePaola (Penguin Putnam, 1983)

The Legend of the Indian Paintbrush by Tomie dePaola (Penguin Putnam, 1988)

Let's Fly from A to Z by Doug Magee and Robert Newman (Cobblehill Books, 1992)

Lightning! by Lorraine Jean Hopping (Scholastic, Inc., 1999)

Lilly's Purple Plastic Purse by Kevin Henkes (Greenwillow Books, 1996)

Little Critter's This Is My School by Mercer Mayer (Golden Books, 1990)

Lizards by Carolyn MacLulich (HarperCollins, 2000)

The Magic School Bus: At the Waterworks by Joanna Cole (Scholastic, Inc., 1990)

The Magic School Bus: In the Time of the Dinosaurs by Joanna Cole (Scholastic, Inc., 1994)

The Magic School Bus: Inside a Beehive by Joanna Cole (Scholastic, Inc., 1996)

The Magic School Bus: Inside the Earth by Joanna Cole (Scholastic, Inc., 1987)

The Magic School Bus: Inside the Human Body by Joanna Cole (Scholastic, Inc., 1989)

The Magic School Bus: Inside a Hurricane by Joanna Cole (Scholastic, Inc., 1995)

The Magic School Bus: Lost in the Solar System by Joanna Cole (Scholastic, Inc., 1990)

The Magic School Bus: On the Ocean Floor by Joanna Cole (Scholastic, Inc., 1992)

Marvin K. Mooney Will You Please Go Now! by Dr. Seuss (Random House, 1972)

[Children's Books Cited]

Meet My Grandmother: She's a Supreme Court Justice by Lisa Tucker McElroy (Millbrook Press, 2001)

Meet the Barkers: Morgan and Moffat Go to School by Tomie dePaola (Puffin Books, 2003)

The Memory String by Eve Bunting (Clarion Books, 2000)

Monarch Butterfly by Gail Gibbons (Holiday House, 1991)

The Monster at the End of this Book by Jon Stone (Random House, 2000)

Mother's Day Mess by Karen Gray Ruelle (Holiday House, 2003)

Mouse Cookies by Laura Numeroff and Felicia Bond (Laura Gerringer, 1995)

Mouse Soup by Arnold Lobel (HarperCollins, 1977)

Mouse Tales by Arnold Lobel (HarperCollins, 1972)

Mrs. Katz and Tush by Patricia Polacco (Dell Dragonfly Books, 1992)

Mrs. Mack by Patricia Polacco (Philomel, 1998)

My Great-Aunt Arizona by Gloria Houston (HarperTrophy, 1997)

My Rotten Redheaded Older Brother by Patricia Polacco (Aladdin Paperbacks, 1994)

The Mysteries of Harris Burdick by Chris Van Allsburg (Houghton Mifflin, 1984)

Nana Upstairs & Nana Downstairs by Tomie dePaola (Penguin Putnam Books, 1973)

Night Tree by Eve Bunting (Voyager Books, 1991)

Now One Foot, Now the Other by Tomie dePaola (G. P. Putnam's Sons, 1980)

Oliver Button Is a Sissy by Tomie dePaola (Voyager, 1990)

One Fish Two Fish Red Fish Blue Fish by Dr. Seuss (Random House, 1981)

[Children's Books Cited]

Our Teacher's Having a Baby by Eve Bunting (Clarion Books, 1992)

Owen by Kevin Henkes (Greenwillow Books, 1993)

Owl at Home by Arnold Lobel (HarperTrophy, 1982)

Passover by Miriam Nerlove (Albert Whitman, 1992)

Penguins! by Gail Gibbons (Holiday House, 1998)

Picnic at Mudsock Meadow by Patricia Polacco (Trumpet, 1992)

A Picture Book of Abraham Lincoln by David A. Adler (Holiday House, 1989)

A Picture Book of Amelia Earhart by David A. Adler (Holiday House, 1998)

A Picture Book of Benjamin Franklin by David A. Adler (Holiday House, 1990)

A Picture Book of Christopher Columbus by David A. Adler (Holiday House, 1991)

A Picture Book of Dwight David Eisenhower by David A. Adler (Holiday House, 1992)

A Picture Book of Eleanor Roosevelt by David A. Adler (Holiday House, 1991)

A Picture Book of Florence Nightingale by David A. Adler (Holiday House, 1992)

A Picture Book of Frederick Douglas by David A. Adler (Holiday House, 1993)

A Picture Book of George Washington by David A. Adler (Holiday House, 1989)

A Picture Book of George Washington Carver by David A. Adler (Holiday House, 1999)

A Picture Book of Harriet Beecher Stowe by David A. Adler (Holiday House, 2003)

A Picture Book of Harriet Tubman by David A. Adler (Holiday House, 1992)

A Picture Book of Jackie Robinson by David A. Adler (Holiday House, 1994)

[Children's Books Cited]

A Picture Book of Lewis and Clark by David A. Adler (Holiday House, 2003)

A Picture Book of Martin Luther King, Jr. by David A. Adler (Holiday House, 1989)

A Picture Book of Robert E. Lee by David A. Adler (Holiday House, 1994)

A Picture Book of Rosa Parks by David A. Adler (Holiday House, 1993)

A Picture Book of Sacagawea by David A. Adler (Holiday House, 2000)

A Picture Book of Sojourner Truth by David A. Adler (Holiday House, 1994)

A Picture Book of Thomas Jefferson by David A. Adler (Holiday House, 1990)

Pink and Say by Patricia Polacco (Philomel, 1994)

Planet Earth, Inside Out by Gail Gibbons (Mulberry Books, 1990)

Play Ball, Amelia Bedelia by Peggy Parrish (HarperTrophy, 1996)

Polar Bears by Gail Gibbons (Holiday House, 1995)

The Popcorn Book by Tomie dePaola (Holiday House, 1984)

Purim by Miriam Nerlove (Albert Whitman, 1992)

Purple, Green and Yellow by Robert Munsch (Annick Press, 1992)

Rabbits by Gail Gibbons (Holiday House, 1999)

Rechenka's Eggs by Patricia Polacco (Penguin Putnam Books for Young Readers, 1996)

The Relatives Came by Cynthia Rylant (Antheneum, 2001)

Rescue Helicopters by Hal Rogers (Child's World, 2000)

Rhyme Time Valentine by Nancy Poydar (Holiday House, 2003)

[Children's Books Cited]

Roxaboxen by Alice McLerran (Lothrop Lee and Shepard, 1991)

Seven Spools of the Thread: A Kwanzaa Story by Angela Shelf Medearis (Albert Whitman, 2000)

Shabbat by Miriam Nerlove (Albert Whitman, 1998)

Sheila Rae, the Brave by Kevin Henkes (Mulberry Books, 1996)

Sheila Rae's Peppermint Stick by Kevin Henkes (HarperFestival, 2001)

Slinky, Scaly Snakes by Jennifer Dussling (DK Publishing, 1998)

Small Pig by Arnold Lobel (HarperTrophy, 1986)

Smoky Night by Eve Bunting (Voyager Books, 1994)

The Snowy Day by Ezra Jack Keats (Viking, 1981)

Some Birthday by Patricia Polacco (Simon and Schuster, 1991)

Song and Dance Man by Karen Ackerman (Knopf, 1988)

Spiders by Carolyn B. Otto (Scholastic, Inc., 2002)

Spiders by Gail Gibbons (Holiday House, 1993)

The Stranger by Chris Van Allsburg (Houghton Mifflin, 1986)

Strega Nona by Tomie dePaola (Scholastic, Inc., 1975)

Strega Nona: Her Story by Tomie dePaola (Puffin Books, 1996)

Suddenly! by Colin McNaughton (Voyager Books, 1998)

The Sweetest Fig by Chris Van Allsburg (Houghton Mifflin, 1993)

Teach Us, Amelia Bedelia by Peggy Parrish (Scholastic, Inc., 2003)

[Children's Books Cited]

Ten Apples Up On Top! by Theo. LeSieg (Random House, 1961)

Terrific Trains by Tony Mitton (Scholastic, Inc., 2000)

Thank You, Amelia Bedelia by Peggy Parrish (HarperTrophy, 1993)

Thank You, Mr. Falker by Patricia Polacco (Philomel, 1998)

Thanksgiving by Miriam Nerlove (Albert Whitman, 1990)

Thanksgiving Day by Gail Gibbons (Holiday House, 1983)

There's a Wocket in My Pocket! by Dr. Seuss (Random House, 1974)

This Is a Pumpkin by Abby Levine (Albert Whitman, 1997)

This Is the Turkey by Abby Levine (Albert Whitman, 2000)

The Three Pigs by David Weisner (Clarion Books, 2001)

Thunder Cake by Patricia Polacco (The Putnam & Grosset Group, 1997)

Train to Somewhere by Eve Bunting (Clarion Books, 1996)

A Turkey for Thanksgiving by Eve Bunting (Clarion Books, 1995)

Twisters by Kate Hayden (DK Publishers, 2000)

Uncle Elephant by Arnold Lobel (HarperTrophy, 1986)

Valentine's Day by Gail Gibbons (Holiday House, 1985)

Valentine's Day by Miriam Nerlove (Albert Whitman, 1992)

The Wall by Eve Bunting (Clarion Books, 1990)

Weather by Melissa Getzoff (Troll Communications, 1996)

[Children's Books Cited]

Weather Forecasting by Gail Gibbons (Aladdin, 1993)

Weather Words and What They Mean by Gail Gibbons (Holiday House, 1992)

The Wednesday Surprise by Eve Bunting (Clarion Books, 1989)

A Weekend with Wendell by Kevin Henkes (Mulberry Books, 1995)

Wemberly Worried by Kevin Henkes (Greenwillow Books, 2000)

What Makes the Weather by Janet Palazzo (Troll Communications, 1989)

What Will the Weather Be? by Jean Dewitt (Scott Foresman, 1993)

Whatever the Weather by Karen Wallace (DK Publishers, 1999)

Wheels, Wings, and Other Things by Monica Hughes and Barbara Hunter (Rigby, 2000)

When I Get Bigger by Mercer Mayer (Golden Books, 1986)

When I Was Young in the Mountains by Cynthia Rylant (E. P. Dutton, 1993)

Why Is the Sky Blue? by Marian B. Jacobs (Rosen, 1998)

The World of Ants by Melvin Berger (Newbridge, 1993)